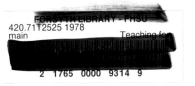

E DUE

WITHDRAWN

Teaching for Literacy:
Reflections on the Bullock Report

Editors:
Frances R. A. Davis
and
Robert P. Parker, Jnr

Agathon Press, Inc. New York

Set in 11 on 13 Imprint and printed by
Latimer Trend & Company Ltd, Plymouth
for Agathon Press, Inc.
150 Fifth Avenue, New York, USA
Made in Great Britain

Contents

Acknowledgments

We want to express our gratitude to several people who contributed greatly to the preparation and final shape of this book. To Monroe Cohen who gave us every encouragement; to Burton Lasky, formerly with Agathon Press who saw the value in such a book; to Earl Davis for countless hours of proof reading and moral support; and to Barbara Hoover for her patience in typing large portions of the manuscript.

Foreword

James Britton

The three years or so that separated the first meeting of the
Bullock Committee from the publication of its Report in 1975
certainly provided me with a learning experience, perhaps a
major one. Yet I do not relish the task of trying to say precisely
what it is I learnt in that time.

I have, of course, a good deal of lumber: copies of papers
produced by Committee members or presented to them; photo-
stats of existing publications someone thought they ought to pay
heed to; minutes of fifty-four meetings of the Committee and
some twenty-five meetings of its subcommittees; successive
drafts leading up to the final version of the Report; bundles of
evidence submitted in writing, some of it brilliant, some fanatical,
some blindingly obvious, and a lot of it modestly helpful to us at
the time. I have called it lumber, but I preserve it with care since
one day I may be able to turn the lumber into learning. Mean-
while, what do I know I have learnt?

I learnt, over many months, to question the possibility of
affecting what goes on in schools through the particular means
we were employing, that is through the agency of a government-
sponsored committee. It was at times exhilarating to find that
ideas long nurtured in the various factions members belonged to
had suddenly acquired the stamp of official approval, had been
uttered, so to speak, in the establishment voice. But then followed a doubt as to whether the act of official formulation was in
fact a further and enhancing stage in the long process of nurturing, or whether it might be a step in reverse. If nurturing an idea
means getting more of the appropriate people to think about it
for themselves, might its transmogrification into official dogma
result in *less* of that thinking, more of a taking for granted?
Ironically, one of the very ideas that gained this promotion into
the establishment is itself a relevant principle to apply at this
point: the Report urges teachers to take more account of students'

'intentions' as a means of facilitating their learning. The context is that of learning to write:

> The solution lies in a recognition on the part of teachers that a writer's intention is prior to his need for techniques. The teacher who aims to extend the pupil's power as a writer must therefore work first upon his intentions, and *then* upon the techniques appropriate to them. . . . Spontaneity then becomes capable of surviving the transition from artlessness to art; or in plainer terms, of supporting a writer in his search for new techniques appropriate to his novel intentions. (p. 104)

But if nurturing an idea about teaching and learning (such as that particular one) involves the generating of new insights and hence novel intentions on the part of teachers, is it not possible that an officially published brief injunction might appear to the teacher as no more than *other people's* intentions with respect to his behaviour?

I learnt to raise this question, but not to answer it. My doubts were not resolved when, after a brief round of debate in 'launching' the Bullock Report in this country, I went to Australia and attended a conference in which teachers and advisers and researchers were discussing the problems of 'language across the curriculum'. I discovered that a great deal of activity, of the 'nurturing' kind, was going on in many parts of the Australian Commonwealth, and I thought that maybe they were fortunate in *not* having an injunction laid at the door of every school to produce a 'language policy for the whole curriculum'. Such an injunction, at its most misunderstood, might result in no more than a concerted witch-hunt against bad spelling and punctuation!

Secondly, I have learnt something about the way people's theories relate to their practices. In a sense this is obvious and familiar enough, but confrontation regularly over a period with consistent differences between the way people behave and the way their theories (presumably) *explain* and *justify* that behaviour to themselves I did find illuminating. The matter is far more complex than the proverbial distinction between 'do as I say' and 'do as I do'. For example, someone who adheres to a conventional behaviourist theory of learning may consistently behave, as a learner and as a teacher – or, in the situation of a committee, in the strategies he uses to expound his own views and explore other people's – in ways that are far more adequately explained in terms of a humanistic, cognitive theory. Alternatively, someone who justifies the classroom practices in his school by appealing to humanistic psychology may seem consistently to employ techniques of reinforcement, positive and negative, in order to get the better of an argument. It follows that we cannot make a simple judgment upon the value of anyone's contribution to the educational enterprise; and that too ready recognition of educational 'factions' may obscure many of the subtleties of likeness and difference. (To accept 'neutrality' at this point as a way of solving the dilemma would be a gross misconstruction: rather we are forced back to reaffirm the importance for all practitioners of arriving at theories that will empower rather than frustrate their behaviour.) It is my overriding impression that teaching experience – the repeated intuitive response to teaching/learning confrontations – makes teachers much more alike in their behaviour than in the theories they rely on to explain and justify that behaviour. But the simple logic of behaviourist learning theory has an obvious appeal to administrators because it makes evaluating, accounting and planning seem much more feasible; and administrators, by persuading or overriding teachers, have frequently succeeded in having such theory applied in the classroom. Where this happens, 'intentions' (as we envisaged them above) have no place in the programme, and the gap thus created we feverishly try to fill under the label of 'motivation'. In my view, accountability should be truly seen as the teacher taking full responsibility for the behaviour of the daily confrontation; and only a learning theory that adequately explains both his successes and his failures in the confrontation can help him discharge that responsibility.

My experience on the Bullock Committee, then, serves to underline the importance to teachers of a rationale, a theory that is consistent with and supportive of their practices. It provides us with a running code of operational principles, a way of monitoring our own practice, a way of effectively influencing other people and defending our own position.

I learnt also a good deal about the nature of compromise and the ways in which it operates. The Chairman, Sir Alan Bullock (now Lord Bullock), repeatedly reminded members that they must resist the temptation to overstate their views for the sake of reducing the scope of wilful misinterpretation. It is a fair point: wilful misinterpretation is always possible and it is pointless to try and guard against it – and worse than pointless if in doing so we distort our views in stating them. And yet there is still a problem: a view that is innocently stated in good faith may be adequate communication to a reader who comes halfway to meet it, but if it is to challenge another reader to *change* his view, it will need to carry conviction by anticipating and countering his objections. Now it must surely be recognized that the language of establishment documents has been evolved in order, amongst other things, to give as little unnecessary offence as possible. This results very often in a general air of lack of conviction. In the case of the Bullock Report, I believe its establishment status, the size and diversity of views of the membership, the amount of data it was expected to handle, all militated against the production of a forthright and convincing document. Compare it, for example, with the Report of the Study Group on Linguistic Communication to the National Institute of Education (USA) (Miller 1974): in session at the same time as the Bullock Committee and working in the same field, ten members were able in less than two weeks to prepare a report that carries more conviction and more daring speculation than was possible in the full-scale British enquiry, with twenty members working for two years.

The compromise that creeps into the finally edited wording of a committee document is perhaps the most difficult kind to control. An individual writer's words will very often both make his statement and at the same time, by means which it may be difficult to identify, make clear the direction from which the statement is 'projected'. For the sake of stylistic uniformity, the corporate document must sacrifice these individual signposts and take on instead the tones of an echoing oracle, coming from everywhere. After making allowances for some inevitable toning down, however, it is disturbing to find that a member's original draft may undergo compromising amendment such as the following. In the chapter on writing, at a point where the relation between language study and performance in writing is being considered, the original draft ran:

> Explicit rules and facts about language (that is to say the outcomes of other people's studies) probably have direct practical value to the language user only insofar as they solve problems in the tasks he is engaged on, or insofar as he is able to reconstruct for himself the analysis that led to the rule. It is the neglect of these limiting conditions that has led to much profitless language work in schools.

But the version finally approved by the Committee has clearly lost *en route* something of its directed thrust:

> Explicit rules and facts about language, that is to say the outcomes of other people's studies, have direct practical value to a pupil when (a) they solve particular problems in the tasks he is engaged on, or (b) he is able to reconstruct for himself the analysis that led to the rule. (p. 162)

I believe the Bullock Committee was fortunate in that this kind of drafting drift into compromise was not a frequent occurrence, and I would add that these should be judged alongside a sense of amazement that with so vast an input to interpret and so diverse a company of interpreters the Report ever got written at all!

Where such changes did occur, however, they were symptomatic of a much more general and far-reaching impulsion to compromise inherent in the whole situation. When Mrs Margaret Thatcher, as Minister of Education, set up the Committee of Enquiry into Reading and the Use of English, she selected as members representatives of the principal factions, or schools of thought, in the field and chose a neutral chairman – someone not already credited with views on the controversial issues since his expertise lay in a different field. One must suppose that Mrs Thatcher believed that what was important about the learning and teaching of the mother tongue lay at a deeper level, was more fundamental, than the issues over which people disagreed. In effect, she called together a disparate crew and told them she fervently hoped for a unanimous report. The Chairman, Sir

Alan Bullock, seems to have shared this view, since from beginning to end he worked to have the Committee produce a report which all members would sign. He succeeded, though the substantial list of reservations itemised by one member after signing somewhat vitiates the success. In any case, its cost in time and effort was enormous: a majority view, as distinct from a unanimous one, would have been far easier to reach and would have constituted a document with more conviction. In other words, the situation created had the effect of ensuring that compromise was built into the production from the outset. I emerged from the experience more convinced than ever that the issues over which there are sharply conflicting views about English teaching are the fundamental, formative issues. Harold Rosen (1975), in a published critique of the Report, makes the point very well. He writes:

It is not difficult to detect behind the Report's fair and mostly dispassionate tones the fact that in matters of language and the teaching of English in particular the battle-lines have been drawn. However faint they may seem there is no doubt that the fiercest debates are between those who believe in carefully constructed linear programmes, buttressed by claims for sequence, system and structure, and those who believe that development in language can only be achieved by working in a much more flexible and open-ended way.

It was when the approved versions of the various chapters finally came together for the first time that I realized the full effect of the thousand and one particular compromises that had been made throughout the drafting. The picture that emerged seemed to me altogether too firmly drawn, as though the problems did not exist to which the Committee had no answer. The compromises, in other words, had been reductive in effect, an avoidance of many of the real complexities; what had been lost was precisely a sense of openness and flexibility. It was at this stage that I drafted my own reservations, which became, in the course of the ensuing argument, an appended 'Note of Extension' to the Report.

A few months after the Report was published, I retired and spent the next two years teaching mainly in Canada, with visits to the States and Australia. Back in England now, in 1977, I must say that the Bullock Report begins to look like a beacon that shines brighter and brighter as the skies around it darken. Amid all the talk of 'literacy' and 'evaluation', both very narrowly conceived, can it survive to keep before us a more enlightened view of language and learning? The darkening skies are certainly not a local phenomenon, but belong at least to the whole Western world: inflation brings anxiety, and anxiety will tend to reduce the number of factors we are willing to take into account in making a judgment. In a time of shrinking perspectives, educational perspectives are particularly vulnerable if for no other reason than that schools constitute a large part of the national budget.

I do not believe that 'enlightened education' (meaning, in its true sense, 'progressive education') is part of any bandwagon, or fashion cycle, or pendulum swing; it is a slowly growing movement with philosophical roots way back in the past and pragmatic roots deep in the intuitive wisdom of the most success-ful teachers today. It has not been tried and found wanting: as the Bullock Committee Survey was able to indicate, it has as yet barely achieved a foothold in the schools of this country.[1] I doubt whether there was ever a time when it was more important, or more difficult, than it is today to keep these ideas alive. I hope the Bullock Report, despite all my earlier reservations, will finally prove its worth as an aid and support to those who are trying to do so.

It is for this reason that I welcome the idea of this book, and the variety of views expressed by its contributors.

REFERENCES

DES (1975) *A Language for Life* (Bullock Report) London: Her Majesty's Stationery Office

MILLER, G. A. (1974) (Ed.) *Linguistic Communication: Perspectives for Research* Newark, Delaware: International Reading Association

ROSEN, H. (1975) (Ed.) *Language and Literacy in our Schools: Some Appraisals of the Bullock Report* London: University of London Institute Studies in Education 1

NOTES

1 See Bullock, the tables on pp. 373 and 376 (where 'vertical grouping' may be taken as the formal indicator of a 'progressive school', whereas the data reported show little departure from traditional methods).

1   The context of the Bullock Report

Frances R. A. Davis

The Bullock Committee presented their survey of the state of literacy learning and teaching in a Report entitled *A Language for Life*. Following the tradition of such earlier investigations as the Hadow and Plowden Committees, the Bullock Committee was a major effort to bring together summary information about schools and their educational practices. In addition, it raised literacy issues of great import.

Because of its reflection of current language learning and teaching practices and its delineation of literacy issues, the Report became a stimulus for discussion and dialogue among parents and professional educators throughout England. The impact of these discussions and dialogues cannot be measured directly, but the fact of their occurrence is a promising sign. For schools already approaching literacy learning and teaching in the ways the Committee recommended, the Report articulated and solidified their thought about those practices; for those not already following the recommendations, it became an opportunity to reflect upon and justify the programmes they were supporting.

Though the generalizations and recommendations in the Report are based upon evidence from British schools, they have implications for all those interested in language instruction in English. As such, they are equally as important for American educators as they are for the British. The complex issues involved in literacy have tremendous political, social, and intellectual ramifications, and both English-speaking countries have deep concerns about these and the state of language teaching in their schools. The issues cut to the heart of our lives: the ways in which we live and teach; the ways we talk; and the ways we read and write. For those of us in America, the Committee's investigation and its conclusions are significant; these, too, are our issues. Despite the cultural differences between the two countries, we hold in common many of the same problems of language learning and teaching.

The British and American educators who were chosen to write papers for this volume do not deal directly with the literacy issues raised by the Committee, nor do they simply provide a critical analysis of the Report. Rather, through the example of their own research and/or teaching experiences, each author draws inferences from the issues in the light of American and British concerns about language learning throughout the life span. In doing this, the authors provide insight into both their own work and its relationship to literacy teaching, and its relationship to the specific issues raised in the Bullock Report. They extend the Committee's recommendations for further discussion on both sides of the Atlantic.

BACKGROUND OF THE BULLOCK COMMITTEE AND ITS REPORT

The Bullock Committee was appointed as a response to the British public's alarm over the published results of a survey concerning the state of reading standards in their schools. The survey, *The Trends of Reading Standards* conducted by Start and Wells (1973), reported a drop in the reading and writing abilities of school children. These results, published by the prestigious National Foundation for Educational Research (NFER), were questioned by some in England on the basis of the methodology employed in the study. Nevertheless, the British government which assumes responsibility for teaching in the schools immediately responded. Margaret Thatcher, then Secretary of State for Education and Science, appointed the Committee to study the charge of declining standards. The Committee, chaired by Sir Alan Bullock, a former vice-chancellor of Oxford University, was specifically formed to enquire into the teaching of reading, and it became known as the Bullock Committee.

In compiling the information about schools and literacy teaching, the Committee relied upon survey results from a random sample of 1,415 primary schools and 392 secondary schools. Other information came from written evidence presented to the Committee by individuals and organizations, from personal interviews with a substantial number of persons, and from specially prepared papers authored by a number of educators. Visits were made by Committee members to 100 schools, twenty-one colleges of education, and six reading or language centres in various parts of the country.

> These visits . . . gave members the opportunity to see different methods of teaching and organization and above all to talk to a large number of teachers in their classrooms. The Committee also studied at first and second hand, the practice of certain other English-speaking countries. Evidence was received from Scotland, Canada and the United States. . . . (p. xxxiv)

Through its examination of a range of issues in language and literacy teaching in educational settings, the Committee did more than evaluate a specific curricular area or educational system. The title selected for the Report, *A Language for Life*, reflects, rather, an emphasis on an underlying language philosophy drawn from current psychological and educational theory.

> We believe that language competence grows incrementally, through an interaction of writing, talking, reading, and experience, the body of resulting work forming an organic whole. (p. 7)

Thus, in the process of their investigation, the Bullock Committee agreed that reading could not be separated from other language uses; reading must be considered within the context of a total language system.

The change in focus from one centred on a single facet of language learning to one encompassing reading *and* other uses of language was paralleled by an enlargement of the Committee's original brief. The scope of the study changed from one limited to the schooling years to a study of language learning from early ages to adulthood. As a result, the investigation was expanded to include the home and other factors related to individual language learning which do not involve the school *per se*. Thus, language development was considered along a continuum of learning in many media before, during, and after school life. This overall unified language approach taken by the Committee is reflected in the organization of the published Report. The Committee refers to this in the Foreword of the Report.

It would have been a simple matter to deal separately with language, taking it right through the age range, and then to have done the same for reading. It would have been equally simple to divide the Report into separate sections for the primary and secondary years, each containing every aspect for the subject as it related to the needs of that particular age group. However, both these methods would have conflicted with the principle that reading, writing, talking and listening should be treated as a unity, and that there should be unbroken continuity across the years. (p. xxxv)

Because of this organization the Report became a comprehensive survey of language uses not only during the school years, but from infancy and preschool through the primary and secondary school years to adulthood.

Investigation of a total language system which operates within and outside of schools gave the Committee an expanded perspective of literacy learning and teaching. They dealt with many complex issues, but in response to the original charge of declining standards they reported that although literacy standards were not as high as might be desired, there was no evidence that they had 'fallen' over recent years. Discussing the matter of standards and the ambiguity inherent in assessment, the Committee noted:

There is no convincing evidence available, and most opinions depend very largely upon subjective impressions. These are not to be dismissed out of hand, but we have already shown how difficult it is to make valid comparisons with the past. We have also remarked that any speculation about standards all too frequently relates them to a particular kind of teaching. We received many letters which suggested that 'creativity' is now reverenced and that 'formal' work has virtually been banished. . . . Our survey gives no evidence of a large body of teachers committed to the rejection of basic skills and not caring who knows it. (p. 6)

In refuting the NFER 1973 survey results, the Bullock Committee also found support in a critical review of studies of reading achievement. This review of six studies by Burke and Lewis (1976) criticized the Start and Wells survey for reporting its literacy figures without allowing for the influx of West Indian and Pakistani children between 1964 and 1970, and for describing a no increase of reading ability as an actual decrease in ability. Further, the Burke-Lewis review called attention to the large number of schools which refused to participate in the Start and Wells survey which made the results even less reliable.

The recommendations presented in the Bullock Report are based upon a thorough examination of existing practices and have already had a significant impact on language teaching and learning in Britain. Working parties of teachers all over the country have read selected parts of the Report and met to discuss them. The Schools Council/University of London Writing Across the Curriculum Project and the National Association for the Teaching of English (NATE) have published responses to various aspects of the Report, as has another combined group of teachers and teacher educators.

The difficulties faced in translating the Committee's recommendations into action, however, are great. Mike Torbe comments on this problem in the Preface to the NATE (1977) *Guidelines*.

> The process of devising and implementing such a policy [Language across the Curriculum] is very complex, and no one knows the best way to go about it. What is clear is that it is a substantially different process from putting new materials into use in a school, or to changing from streaming (ability grouping) to a mixed-ability teaching.

Continued discussion is necessary, therefore, to help shape these processes and implement the suggestions of the Bullock Committee in England. A reflection back to Britain from an American vantage point may aid in providing a clearer understanding of the issues involved and of the very practical problem of implementation.

IMPORTANCE OF THE BULLOCK REPORT FOR AMERICAN EDUCATORS
The concern for the quality of literacy education expressed in

England by the appointment and work of the Bullock Committee is one shared by Americans. Our high school and college faculties bemoan their students' lack of ability in using the English language, and parents of these students are critical of the school's competence in teaching language. For the most part these parents feel that the schools have the responsibility for the education of their children, and they expect them to do whatever is necessary. In some cases they have been belatedly disappointed. At least two legal suits have been filed charging that a student was graduated from a public high school without being able to read or write effectively.

Test results also suggest further evidence of inadequate language learning by students. Scores on the verbal portion of the Scholastic Aptitude test given by the College Entrance Examination Board are reported to have dropped over the last few years, and the National Assessment of Educational Progress (NAEP) test results support these findings among the thirteen to seventeen year old age group. Scores on reading and writing tests for this age group indicate either no change or a drop in literate abilities occurring over a four-year span from 1971 to 1975. All scores except those for functional literacy were lower in 1975 than they were four years earlier. Particularly evident was the drop in scores for the writing-coherency task.

These test results are discouraging. Even the more positive NAEP reports that nine year old children's scores in both reading and writing had improved during this same four-year span, with the scores of black children in all three age levels (nine, thirteen and seventeen) making significant gains, does not provide many people with great encouragement. Our fears that our children are not being adequately prepared to function in today's world are not easily dispelled.

The school as an institution, many charge, is not as effective as it should be in teaching literacy. These feelings of inadequacy are further supported by movements towards greater accountability in all areas of American life – from consumerism to affirmative action. Educational manifestations of these movements are such concepts as criterion teaching, performance-based teacher education, state-wide testing programmes, and the establishment in certain states of minimum standards of competency for high school graduation. These practices developed as responses to our need to educate masses of people expeditiously in functional literacy and computation. Nearly all of these practices imply the provision of tightly controlled, systematic instruction for the learner. The need for a basic education is acknowledged as essential by the planners of all these programmes; but conversely there has also been a call for more humanistic approaches to learning. Basic means something to persons holding either of these views, and this indicates it has different meanings for different people. However it is meant, and however the concept is applied, there is no doubt that 'back to basics' is currently a strong educational movement in America.

In the differing ideas that people hold about what is basic to education, the first things that most consider to be important are reading, writing, and arithmetic – the taking in of language, the expressing of it, and the computation of relationships about it. Language, then, seems to be a crucial aspect of 'basics'. The meanings that basic education encompasses, and the matters of standards and assessment that it emphasizes are important and do need continuing examination. One aspect of an examination of basics should be a review of the attitudes we hold towards the learning and use of language. A thoughtful and dispassionate look at an investigation of the state of literacy teaching in another English-speaking country may aid us in examining our own problems. In doing so, we may gain a fresh perspective on our questions about language learning and teaching: our own state of literacy teaching.

LITERACY ISSUES RAISED IN THE BULLOCK REPORT
The issues that the Report explores fall into five categories:

1 methods and materials of learning and teaching literacy
2 acquisition and development of language in children with atypical behaviour or divergent language
3 standards of competence in, and the assessment of, language
4 preservice and inservice training of teachers
5 school hierarchy and its relationship to internal organization, parents, and those in professions other than education.

In their Report, the Committee did not venture beyond reporting on practice and developing recommendations in each of these areas. Any implications that might be drawn from their treatment of the issues are left to the reader.

Underlying these five basic issues are two divergent points of view about the psychological and linguistic development of children which arise from two fundamentally different views of learning. The Report is comprehensive in reviewing both the Piagetian developmental viewpoint which considers language and learning to be dynamically interrelated with the actions of learners and the view that language is an entity in itself, an object to be polished and perfected, through teaching, according to some external standard of performance. That the Report leans towards the developmental point of view is evident in its emphasis on a holistic approach to the various facets of language and language teaching. The Report gave emphasis to language as a total system in the service of other intellectual endeavours.

The role of language
The unique role language plays in 'generating knowledge' was considered as 'producing new forms of behaviour that typifies human existence and distinguishes it from that of all other creatures'. (p. 47) Man as a symbol-using species can create an inner representation of the world and can construct a past and a future. All these abilities are mirrored in and implemented by language. While emphasizing this, the Committee also avoided the usual controversies about language and thought relationships.

> ... there is no need to enter this controversy, since it is enough to state what would be generally agreed: (a) that higher processes of thinking are normally achieved by the interaction of a child's language behaviour with his other mental and perceptual powers; and (b) that language behaviour represents the aspect of his thought processes most accessible to outside influences, including that of the teacher. (p. 49)

The relationship thus perceived between language and thought led the Committee to their position on the equality of the modes of language. Reading and listening, the receptive modes, were not thought of as more vital than the expressive modes, writing and speaking. At the same time, this equality of relationships among language functions was not presented as a freedom to express without control. The Committee implied an active expressive learner rather than a passive receiving learner. Learning, for the Committee, was considered to require more than a 'laying on' of information to the student by an outside force; learning was to require a response by the student as an active interpreter of new information in relationship to his or her previously formed ideas about the world.

Not every member of the Committee agreed with the concept which equalized the importance of the four modes of language. A dissenting view was written, and was included with the published Report. The dissenting member suggested that a more particular emphasis be placed on the receptive modes of reading and listening in opposition to the productive modes of writing and talking. This writer also subscribed to the more traditional language standards: strong basic skill preparation; structured class activities incorporating creative action, but not shaped by them; and grouping according to ability. Learning, from his point of view, seems accomplished best by an outside force pushing towards the student rather than by an active learner working from within himself.

The dissenter was not alone in viewing language learning in this way. Throughout the Report the Committee acknowledged that many people feel a need for structured language learning; and, among other traditions, the learning of 'basic skills' by drill or other methods is necessary. Other critical comments about the Report charge that the issues were obscured by its sheer bulk, and others voice concern that the inclusiveness of the recommendations make it possible to find substantiation and support for any possible form of teaching. These people criticize the Report for speaking with two voices. Yet, because the Committee was charged to investigate the current state of instruction in schools, it had to reflect conflicts among existing views. As mentioned earlier, the Committee examined current personal growth theories of language teaching such as those advanced in the Dartmouth Seminar (Dixon 1975) and, on the other hand, the more traditional rule-bound, fragmented view of language teaching also was presented.

Language in the social context
Consideration of the language learning of economically-deprived children from divergent racial backgrounds required the Committee to recognize the interrelatedness of language learning and current social problems. In their investigation of the problem of language standards, they asked what should be required of children from educationally-disadvantaged or non-English-speaking backgrounds. In the matter of bilingualism, the Committee recommended that the native language be retained and strengthened *and* proficient English language developed. For all children, however, the Committee stressed the link between the children's deeply felt, essentially unconscious needs, their experiential backgrounds, and their use of language. On this point, Britton suggested the following in his note of extension to the Report.

> Clearly an individual pupil's needs, whatever his culture group, embrace all these uses, and a teacher's concern for him must reach to them. What is at issue is the teacher's priorities, his timing, his tact in the variety of situations that confront him. (p. 555)

The language uses to which Britton refers are those derived from his theory of language functions: an expressive language of the home appropriate within a culture group; poetic language which refines essential cultural values; and transactional language common across culture groups within a society.

Reading instruction
In considering a total language system and a more equal inter-relatedness of the four modes of language, the Committee rejected the overpowering importance many persons in England and elsewhere place upon separate reading instruction at particular stages in children's lives. The Report recognized that children have individual 'learning-clocks', that all children cannot march to the same drummer in lock-step formation. Reading ability, the Committee argues in the Report, develops over a span of time which differs for individual children and pressure to

finish the teaching of it in one or two years seems inappropriate. Because many children must continue work in reading in the junior school years, even though chronologically older that those children in an infant school, the Committee saw a need for junior teachers to be more knowledgeable about the reading process and reading methods.[1] Clearly the Committee intended to suggest the necessity for a language emphasis at all ages in all areas of the curriculum, and that the teaching of reading should take place in this context rather than separately from it.

Readiness for reading
While pushing children into formal reading instruction was to be avoided in the Committee's view, they suggested that schools should maintain a classroom flexibility which would allow children who enter school with the ability to read the opportunity to do so.

> Children with a mental age of four and a half to five can quite happily learn to read if they are given learning experiences which match their individual needs. There is ample evidence of children learning to read at home well before reaching even this kind of mental age. There is no virtue in denying a child access to early experience of reading, provided that it carries meaning and satisfaction for him. (p 100)

Flexible classrooms were defined as those in which young children were not subjected to drill methods or to structured language schemes (programmes) unless those activities were pleasurable, satisfying and profitable.

Attitudes towards 'readiness' for school activities, particularly those aspects of language use traditionally considered to be important for reading, led the Committee to recommend that teachers help children become ready for school learning rather than passively waiting for them to become ready for teaching. Particularly in reading this emphasis means procedures were recommended which would appraise children's use of language and their special needs in regard to its use. The identification of children with sensory or perceptual handicaps through screening, diagnosis and recording was considered essential. However, the

Committee also noted that data collection was valueless unless appropriate treatment measures could be assumed to follow. The Committee recommended the establishment of clinical or remedial centres providing a comprehensive diagnostic service for every school authority. Further, the Committee was careful to stress that the nature of a child's difficulties must be seen in relation to his entire linguistic development. Societal relationships to language use were noted.

> In conclusion we feel it is important to single out again for emphasis the fact that the majority of the pupils who leave school with an inadequate command of reading come from areas of social and economic depression. The problem is more than one of teaching reading, and a combined effort by social services, teachers and administrators is required over the whole period of a child's school life. (p. 275)

Assessment and evaluation of literacy
The Committee deplored the lack of adequate methods of assessment of literacy learning. Traditional methods of evaluation were considered less valid than they had been in earlier reports such as the NFER 1973 survey. The Bullock Committee indicated that frequently tests reflect only a limited portion of abilities within the total language system, and many of these untested qualities were considered as necessary for competent language use in the contemporary world. Their concerns are similar to those voiced by Americans at this time. The Committee recommended a monitoring scheme of assessment which involves putting together banks of test items ranging widely in the skills to be assessed. 'Light sampling' was suggested where the instruments would be applied relatively frequently to a succession of small samples. In this way, the assessment would affect only a few schools at a time and would result in 'spreading the amount of testing over time distributing the content and skills between pools of questions'. (p. 43)

Teachers and their training
The teacher's role was emphasized throughout the Report. The Committee extended itself to support and encourage the work of teachers in the schools as vital.

If there is one general summarizing conclusion we offer it is that there is nothing to equal in importance the quality and achievement of the individual teacher, to whom most of our suggestions are addressed. All our recommendations are designed to support and strengthen the teachers in the schools, for it is with them that improvements in standards of reading and language must assuredly lie. (p. 513)

The understanding that learning is fashioned in daily classroom activities with a teacher's guidance also led the Committee to recognize the paramount importance of teacher training. The Committee concluded that students in most initial training classes do not receive enough information about language learning and teaching. While two specific programmes were presented as examples of good practice, most teacher preparation was seen as particularly weak in reading-method instruction except in the prereading and early stages of the reading of children. More student training with children also was recommended. Encouraging older students to work with younger children was strongly suggested as being of benefit to both age groups. One strength of this plan was the preparent or preteaching value the experience might have for the older children. This type of preparent training, and other types of direct parent education, were suggested as a way to bridge the communication gap between generations and to provide for a continuity of language use from home to school. The lack of integration between theory and practice at every level of training, as well as in research, was deplored and inservice training was seen as vital. The Committee summed up their recommendations about teacher training by saying:

... during their preservice training all teachers should acquire a more complete understanding of language in education than has ever been required of them in the past. However, we must emphasize that we regard this as only the first stage in a continuing process. ... (p. 343)

THE INTENT AND THE ORGANIZATION OF THIS BOOK
The Bullock Report raises many more issues than I have touched

upon here. As stated earlier in this paper, it is the intention of the contributors of this book to present the issues and clarify some of them from the perspective of their own research and teaching. In doing so, it is hoped that these papers may provide an impetus for further discussions of literacy teaching.

The kind of discussions in which people in Britain have engaged about this Report is not foreign to Americans. Two aspects of the Report and its discussion are unusual, however. In America, educational discussions occur primarily within particular groups of people. For example, educators speak with other educators about important issues, psychologists with psychologists, sociologists with sociologists, parents with parents, and so on. In England educational theorists, researchers, school practitioners, college trainers, parents and others are participating in mutual dialogues. In this way, the Bullock Committee's Report has provided a basis for discussions of literacy teaching among various groups within British school and social strata. This intersocial and interdisciplinary discussion presents a fruitful model for Americans.

The papers selected by the editors for this book are generally arranged in categories suggested by the organization of the original Report. They are written by people experienced and competent in educational research, teacher training and administration and teaching in schools. We deliberately chose a mix of American and British authors as well as a mix of classroom teachers, administrators and university professors. Our intent is to present from inside and outside of schools and from both sides of the Atlantic, discussions of language learning and teaching. Eleanore Kenney speaks about the actual operation of the school she administers and tells us how certain issues of language teaching are approached for special children. Ramin Manovi, F. G. Poole and I present the reactions to Bullock of British teachers and administrators from the primary school years to the secondary years. Mike Torbe, Bryan Newton and Bob Parker share their view of the Report's recommendations as reflected in their own work with teachers on the topic of language across the curriculum. Their papers offer another example of the kind of dialogue that can occur between theorists at the university level and practitioners in schools. We continue to model this kind of dialogue with papers from Margaret Roberts, Joan Tough, and Don Ecroyd, each of whom brings us important ideas about language and literacy from their research and college teaching experiences. Kathryn Miller and Chris Crowest also share their expertise in initial and inservice teacher training.

The kind of descriptive research enquiry the Bullock Report represents is currently not in vogue in America. In this volume we do not mean to suggest an either/or position about the kind of research appropriate for the study of schools. Don Ecroyd's paper calls for a careful analysis of the teaching of language by a 'scientist-teacher', and Bob Parker presents a similar concept when he talks about the teacher's 'action-research' in the classroom. Both of these educators recognize the necessity for bridging the gap between traditional research methodology and classroom practice. The combination of the observational-descriptive tradition which is modelled by the British and the experimental methodology of America, two forms of research which are sometimes opposed, is presented consciously in an attempt to increase the effectiveness of research on literacy teaching.

An effort has been made towards extending the usefulness of the Bullock Report by including information from current American research on language processes. Two very interesting accounts of these research efforts are contributed by Charles Cooper and Don Graves. Hopefully the material provided by these authors will aid both American and British teachers in their search for answers to the questions they have about language learning and literacy teaching. If so, this book will be of benefit to teachers personally and to the children for whom they care.

BIBLIOGRAPHY
BURKE, E. and LEWIS, D. (1976) Standards of reading: a critical review of some recent studies *Educational Research* 17,3
DES (1975) *A Language for Life* (Bullock Report) London: Her Majesty's Stationery Office
DIXON, J. (1975) (third edition) *Growth through English* Champaign, Illinois: National Council of Teachers of English
START, K. and WELLS, B. (1973) *The Trend of Reading Standards* Slough, England: National Foundation for Educational Research

NATE (1977) *Language across the Curriculum: Guidelines for Schools* London: National Association for the Teaching of English/Ward Lock Educational

NOTE

1 The organization of children in British schools is somewhat different than the organization in America. While in America children may attend noncompulsory preschool, they usually enter kindergarten around age five. The elementary school years encompass the approximate ages of six to ten or eleven in six 'grades'. In Britain, children may also attend a noncompulsory preschool, and they may enter the infant school at age four or five depending upon the child's development and the availability of space in classes. The infant years range to about age eight when the child progresses to a junior school. The two schools, the infant and the junior, are considered as the primary school. In some cases they actually are housed in one building, in others there are two separate buildings provided.

2 The language and cognitive development of young children

INTRODUCTION

This section reflects the Bullock Committee's findings and recommendations as they apply to three groups of children: first, infants and their parents; second, the language abilities of young children during early childhood; and third, the language development of the special child. Growth in literacy during these crucial first years of children's lives is important and closely tied to their cognitive development. The interactions that children have with their environment seem to be the key to these developments, and it is discussed in the first two papers as it relates to the various age levels of children and the adults who guide them in learning.

Margaret Roberts draws our attention to the beginning stages in the child's acquisition of language. She suggests that as parents, teachers, and researchers we need to know more about our roles in helping young babies express and communicate their feelings through a wide range of behaviours. The Bullock Report is faulted for not providing guidance for those who are responsible for very young infants. Drawing on the research of Trevarthen, Schaffer, and others, Roberts maintains that the infant is an active learner who stimulates the adult to respond to him. This communicating interaction of infants with adults, which is such a necessary part of the language-acquisition process, evolves through mother and child contact. It is a process that should receive more attention from those responsible for the preparation of young people for parenthood.

Moving from parent education to the training of older children who might become tutors for younger children, Roberts agrees with Bullock that both older and younger children benefit from tutor-learner interaction, but she suggests we frequently do not provide older children with the kind of information they need to profit the most from the experience themselves, or to provide the most valuable experiences for the younger child.

Joan Tough emphasizes the preschool child's language inter-actions at home and during the earliest years of school. She helps us understand the environments which encourage the develop-ment of the child's ability to communicate meaning through language.

Tough's work with children in the classroom has a close con-nection with her own research into the natural ways a child develops meaning in the use of language. She shares some of this research with us, and shows the relationship it has to other British and American studies of children's expressive language. While Tough does not provide us with the details of their work, she discusses the experiences of the Schools Council Com-munication Skills in Early Childhood Project, based at Leeds University. This project staff with the aid of some 1,500 nursery and infant teachers throughout Britain developed special obser-vation and facilitation techniques for teachers to use with children. Their methods are based on a scheme of language use derived from Tough's study of children's language interactions. Eleanore Kenney is Director of the Miriam School, St Louis, Missouri, which provides instruction for children with learning problems. Many of the children are emotionally disturbed as a result of, or in conjunction with, their other problems. The Miriam School also cooperates with classroom teachers in the local school district so that children may benefit from the Miriam programme who actually attend other schools.

Dr Kenney describes Miriam's 'Developmental Learning Programme', carried out jointly with the St Louis Public School District, and helps us understand how public and private schools can cooperate in the education of children. In her paper, Dr Kenney also clarifies for us three different levels of learning dis-orders of children with normal intellectual potential. Importantly, she tells us, children with minor processing disorders develop into children with major learning disorders when the curriculum does not match their developmental pattern of learning. Because the Bullock Report calls only for an identification of problems without differentiating among types of disorders, this thoughtful clarification offers an advancement beyond the Report's scope.

The authors of each of the papers in this section interpret and extend the Bullock Committee's suggestions in light of the developmental growth of young children. Their concern for literacy learning is closely interrelated with the cognitive development of children from infancy to middle-childhood. Information about these interrelationships provides both British and American parents and teachers with material for further thought about literacy learning and teaching.

Provision for language growth in young children

Margaret Roberts

The writer of the introduction to Bullock says, somewhat strangely perhaps, 'Indeed, *we felt it necessary* to begin with the years before a child comes to school and to examine the influence of the home on early language development' (my italics). The writer sounds almost apologetic that the Committee began with the years before a child comes to school. In fact the Report does not begin with language in the early years; it begins with 'Attitudes and Standards', attitudes to the teaching of English and standards of reading.

In view of the enormous amount of material in the Report on the later stages of language development, its thorough examination of language study, and its application to education, it is, perhaps, ungenerous to point out that recent studies of the very young child's language interaction with his social environment are virtually ignored.

The omission of this material should not be exaggerated but in view of what *is* included in Part Two, 'Language in the Early Years', and the very brief reference to language acquisition, the omissions are serious for the student of the early stages of human expression and communication. The exciting research studies, carried out in Britain by people like Schaffer, Trevarthen, Bower (1977), Richards (1973) on the baby's social interaction with his environment in the first year of life, are neglected. Inclusion of these research findings would strengthen Bullock's recommendations about the school's collaboration with parents and others who care for young babies.

I intend to bring together the findings of research in early childhood and the recommendations of Bullock to see how far they match up. One recommendation regarding the need for teachers to study language and language development at initial and inservice level in order to help aids, nursery nurses and parents to help young children needs no qualification. But careful observation of early interaction behaviour between mother and baby, or other care-giver and baby, throws light on young babies' capacity for learning beyond what Bullock has to say.

However, Bullock deals with certain aspects of early childhood which are clearly important. Suggestions for work with parents-to-be and parents of young children are supported by recent findings from psychologists and linguists regarding the capabilities of very young babies. Reports of careful observations and film/video tape recordings indicate that the very young baby is far from being passive and indiscriminating in relation to his surroundings. There is evidence that the new-born baby is pre-adapted for social interaction; as Colin Trevarthen puts it, 'the infant builds a bridge to persons'. But for the bridge to be effective there must be someone to receive the baby's efforts at communication and respond to them.

Trevarthen has begun a detailed examination of infant communication with persons. He writes in *Child Alive* (Lewin 1975) of a project which involves careful filming and subsequent analysis of the acts of two month olds responding to the attentions of other persons. He writes:

We have found activity which is best called 'prespeech' because both the context in which it occurs and its form indicate that it is a rudimentary form of speaking by movements of lips and tongue. These distinctive movements are often made by young infants soundlessly. At other times young babies are very vocal, making a variety of cooing sounds as they move mouth and tongue. We note a specific pattern of breathing with prespeech even when sounds are not made.

Trevarthen goes on to say that he and his colleagues have observed distinctive 'hand-waving' movements that are developmentally related to the gestures and gesticulations of adults in 'eager' and 'graphic' conversation. He writes:

We are now sure that, notwithstanding the importance of cultural development in the formation of language, both of speech and gestures, the foundation for interpersonal communication between humans is 'there' at birth, and is remarkably useful by eight weeks when cognitive and memory processes are just starting on the path to mastery of the world of physical events.

Viewing communication activity as much more complex than any other form of activity of infants at this age, Trevarthen concludes that human intelligence develops as an interpersonal process and that the maturation of consciousness and the ability to act with voluntary control in the physical world is *a product* rather than an ingredient of this process, *a consequence* rather than a cause of understanding between persons.

But clearly infant communication needs a partner and H. R. Schaffer (1971), using frame by frame analysis of films and video tapes of mother-child interaction sequences in the feeding situation, has repeatedly been struck by the turn-taking nature of mother's and baby's vocalizations: 'Mother and baby rarely vocalize at the same time, and the alternation so produced is thus somewhat like a conversation among adults.' Schaffer thinks that the turn-taking is entirely due to the mother's initiative. The baby emits bursts of vocalization and it is left to the mother to fill in the pauses. He thinks that the synchronization of the two sets of responses is entirely due to the mother letting herself be paced by the infant's periodic behaviour.

This interaction between the young baby of two months and his mother, with the mother responding to the baby's communication, develops gradually towards reciprocity. Early interpersonal exchange is later developed in relation to the young baby's interest in objects which can be grasped, brought to the mouth and later manipulated; 'conversation' is related to these activities – an extension of the shared interpersonal world to the world of things and actions. Objects that attract the baby's attention and his reaching/grasping behaviour around four and five months become *shared objects* of interest with familiar adults such as the mother or other care-giver. Trevarthen sees this behaviour of the baby in bringing objects from the outside into the 'conversation' with a familiar adult as a seeking of 'companionship in experience'. Further cognitive and linguistic development of the baby in the second half of his first year is seen to be closely related to his interpersonal experiences in the first six months of life. Briefly Trevarthen summarizes his findings in *Child Alive*: 'Human social intelligence is the result of development of an innate human mode of psychological function that requires transactions with other persons.'

Clearly much of the recent knowledge in this field has led to the questioning of earlier ideas about the young child's early learning. The concept of imitation as the basis of early learning now requires reappraisal. Film records clearly show the mother imitating the baby's facial movements and echoing his sounds. True imitation by the baby seems to follow later as a result of the adult's deliberate attempts to get the baby to imitate. Trevarthen notes that he and his colleagues have rarely seen imitation of the mother's facial movements in babies under six months. On the other hand he writes:

We are impressed with the elaborate and faithful mimicry of the more animated acts of the baby *by the mother*. Apparently *her* imitation is an important part of the normal encouragement to conversational activity by the baby.

Recent experimental studies have shown the emotional effects on an infant when a mother, or other familiar partner, acts irrelevantly. If the partner intentionally witholds all responses and just makes a blank face, not acting in any threatening way, the baby is clearly puzzled and becomes dejected-looking and withdrawn. It would appear that expectations are not met in terms of the partner's response and the baby is disturbed. This evidence of the baby's sensitivity to the quality of interpersonal experience as early as eight to ten weeks emphasizes the importance of continuity in early care-giving in terms of initial attachments. This brings us to a consideration of children who have suffered from a breakdown in continuous intimate mothering, or whose mothering has been of poor quality.

Bullock's approach to this problem is preventive and educative. First, it is to help parents understand the process of language development in their children and to take part in it. Second, it is to develop the skill and knowledge of the nursery and infant teacher both in terms of her measured attention to the child's precise language needs and of her inventiveness in creating situations which bring about their fulfilment.

Before dealing with the practicalities of these two approaches the Report reviews briefly what is known about the way in which a child acquires language and the forces governing how it develops. The study starts at the stage when a child begins to connect two or three words together: between eighteen and twenty-four months. The naming function which precedes this is dealt with cursorily and in an oversimplified way, stressing the 'capacity to imitate his parents'. No mention is made of the child's ability to invent his own naming words such as 'go-goes' for all moving traffic, or 'bib-bon' for all types of food, words spontaneously produced by two children in their second year.

The point is made that the child tends to reproduce the content words which receive stress in normal speech. When the child produces his short two/three word sentences he puts the words in the right order, e.g. 'Daddy come'. He acquires the basic rules of syntax early, placing subject and predicate in their natural relationship. He responds to intonational patterns at a surprisingly early age.

References made to American studies by Brown and Bellugi show the way in which the adult 'opens up the child's area of verbal operation', e.g. the child's two word statement 'Daddy come' is expanded by the mother into, 'Yes, Daddy will be coming home soon'. Mothers were found to be expanding their children's simple utterances nearly a third of the time. However, this is not the whole story. Anyone who has listened to a young child talking knows the inventiveness with which he tries out groups of words he is clearly not directly imitating, e.g. 'Baby other bite balloon, no' from Christy (2.3) after her baby sister burst her balloon by biting it!

Reference is made to American studies illustrating contrasting techniques mothers use to teach their children simple tasks and noting the qualitative differences in language used. The mother from the 'advantaged' home encouraged her child to reflect and to anticipate the consequences of his action in such a way as to avoid error: 'She would do this in language that tended to be abstract and elaborated.' The children from the advantaged homes experienced more sustained conversation within which language was used for a greater variety of functions.

Returning to the role of the parents Bullock quotes witnesses who placed emphasis on actual preparation for parenthood; others preferred to think in less personal terms. In both cases it was suggested that pupils from secondary schools should visit nursery and infant schools, 'where they would learn how to talk with young children in the context of constructive play, perhaps using toys they had made themselves'. An alternative or additional suggestion was that the young children might come to the older children at the secondary school.

Clearly careful preparation is essential; the young people themselves need to be introduced to the work of nursery schools and/ or playgroups through films, video tapes and simple child development literature. They need to know the purpose of the programme at the preschool stage and the selection and provision of toys and equipment. Above all they need guidance on the importance of observation before rushing into conversation with the children who are not already known to them. The idea that young children may be deeply absorbed in their own imaginative play should be considered. Recall and exchange of their own early play experiences have proved useful in sensitizing young people in their approach to children.

I am in agreement with Bullock's recommendation that courses for secondary school children should be broadly based on child development *as an aspect of human development* rather than a narrow mothercraft course. Young people's interest in young children is acknowledged and could be extended to children's language without laying an overt emphasis on personal preparation for parenthood. The Bullock Committee felt that the language development of young children should be set in the wider context of the language human beings use. Films, demonstrations, discussions and practical experience would lead to an awareness of the adult's role in the young child's linguistic and cognitive development: 'This would include a study of the linguistic aspects of relationships, of the questions children ask, and of the value of discussion and explanation in controlling the child's behaviour as against simple prohibition!'

Contact with young children within schools is seen as important and this implies *close cooperation* between teachers. Because there are problems of organization and planning, the teachers of young children may view the prospect with alarm. However, there is no suggestion that large numbers of secondary school pupils would be invading nursery and infant schools. The dominant consideration must be the interests of the young children themselves. Granted this, it should be possible for a pattern of visiting to be devised which would give a large number of pupils *over a period of time* valuable experience. Examples of good practice in this kind of project are given.

The next most productive time to introduce the subject of language development is when young married couples are shortly to become parents. The antenatal clinics are visited by a high percentage of expectant mothers and language development is placed here in the general context of child care in which it can be shown to have an important place. In one clinic expectant mothers were invited to join in with a Mothers' and Toddlers' Club and so gained experience with young children in a relaxed way.

Home-visiting programmes are recommended with the cautionary note that they should be carried out with the greatest delicacy and care. There may be a natural suspicion on the part of the mother that a home visitor is bringing with her a critical attitude to the child's upbringing or the conditions of the home. There may be suspicion of anyone representing authority. The home visitor will need to be 'tolerant and understanding, imposing no judgment and hinting no censure'. The first essential is to win the confidence of the mother and to avoid any suggestion that she might be inadequate in terms of her capacity to nurture her children. Following from this the home visitor will endeavour to set up learning situations which are designed 'to advance the child's linguistic and cognitive development and she will therefore need a good understanding of the processes at work'. A number of home-visiting schemes in the United Kingdom are briefly reviewed, the Halsey West Riding Educational Priority Area Project being particularly successful in developing a sense of partnership with the parents which provides a useful foundation for later home-school collaboration: 'The right kind of relationship with a home visitor can make the prospect of home-school contact a natural one in the mind of the parent.'

Television is seen as having valuable possibilities for increasing parental awareness of their own role in their children's learning activities. Programmes for young children offer to them, and their parents, 'a common experience to talk about'. To achieve this the tone and content must be such that the parents can identify with it. It is suggested that there is room for research into the possibilities of television for the language interaction of parent and child.

There is a note on the more general question of the influence on young children's language of television entertainment programmes. Television reflects the seventies and thus exposes children to a range of idioms and registers. Infants reproduce the terse reporting style of spacemen in a moon landing. They respond to puns, to rhymes and to word play, to jingles and riddles. Language skills used in this kind of verbal play may be very important in early reading. Bullock considers the impact of television and its influence on children's vocabulary, and such aspects of language as accent, idiom and register, well worth further investigation.

In turning to the playgroup, nursery school/class and infant school the Report looks at the role of the teacher in the child's language development. The nursery/infant teacher creates an ordered environment for learning through activity and experience and provides opportunity for reflecting on daily happenings as well as particular personal experiences: 'The teacher encourages the child to relive his experience and embroiders it for him, helping him to draw out of it half-remembered detail.' Talk accompanying activity is seen to be important; whether the activity is concerned with the real world or part of the child's make-believe world. It is seen as an important instrument for learning. A valuable addition to language experience is listening to stories told or read. The hearing of familiar nursery rhymes and singing games provides the shared background or an oral tradition of literature. The children's first drawings are a form of symbolic expression closely linked to thought and feeling; a sympathetic and sensitive adult can encourage the child to 'tell the story' of his drawing which later can provide the important link between drawing, talk and reading. The teacher writing the child's story for him at first provides a model for this new skill.

The question is then explored: is this enough for each and every child? The child from a linguistically impoverished background, it is maintained, requires more carefully planned language experience. In discussing this question several American experiments are examined. The Blank and Solomon one-to-one tutorial programme aiming to 'develop abstract thinking' in the preschool child by encouraging him to discuss situations not present before him is seen as having merit in involving children in explaining and predicting. The Bereiter and Engelmann programme using drill to obtain unison response directed towards developing logical thinking is seen as too narrow in terms of language goals. The Peabody Language Development Kit with its emphasis on group learning of vocabulary, sentence patterns, problem-solving and concept formation gets a divided reaction from English teachers. Those who are critical express preference for programmes which support the teacher's initiative and form an integral part of the child's home-school environment.

Some British experimental programmes designed to extend children's language are examined. These include the Gahagan's games, designed to improve attention, auditory discrimination, speech structure and vocabulary, carried out during a twenty-minute period set aside for these activities every day. The Swansea Compensatory Project working on similar lines directed attention to listening, naming, describing, categorizing, denoting position, sequencing and reasoning. Planned sequences of language experience for children who lack adequate language experience are favoured. The point is made, however, that language programmes should complement and not erode, or replace, normal educational activities and should avoid narrowing the range of language goals.

The participation of parents in the life of the school is welcomed and seen as essentially a cooperative activity. It is recommended that staffing ratios be improved to allow for the appointment of an educational visitor or 'home-liaison teacher' who could work flexibly with the parents and with the children in school, with the emphasis on the liaison teacher's educational rather than social role.

Finally the complexity of the young child's language growth

is stressed. While teachers are concerned to help children 'use words freely' it is necessary to look more deeply into the process of language development. Teachers themselves need to know more about the way language works and what strategies are helpful in meeting children's language needs. I would go further than this and say we need to know more about our role in aiding expression and communication of feeling and thought in a wide range of behaviours, in addition to language, which after all must inevitably summarise and condense our experience; but this would be beyond Bullock's terms of reference.

REFERENCES

BOWER, T. G. R. (1977) *A Primer of Infant Development* Reading, England: W. H. Freeman

RICHARDS, M. P. (Ed.) (1973) *The Integration of a Child into a Social World* Cambridge, England: Cambridge University Press

SCHAFFER, H. R. (1971) *The Growth of Sociability* Harmondsworth, England: Penguin

LEWIN, R. (1975) *Child Alive* London: Temple Smith

Language and learning in the early years and the implications for teaching the youngest

Joan Tough

INTRODUCTION
During recent years the attention of many psychologists, sociologists and educationists has come to focus on the years before school in an attempt to understand why children respond so differently to their school experiences. The results of research into children's achievement in education undertaken during the 1950s and 1960s showed an association between achievement and the socio-economic status of parents. This association is now so well established that no one in Britain disputes the fact. Nor is there much questioning of results that show that the development and use of language are associated on the one hand with educational achievement and intelligence scores, and on the other with the socio-economic status of parents, although the implications that this might have for educating children might be interpreted very differently. Some see differences between the way in which children speak and use language as crucial factors in the child's failure within education, while others see the differences as markers of social class that provide a basis for discrimination on the part of teachers that leads to failure for the child.

There seems to be no doubt that what happens in this area of development can result in advantage or disadvantage for the child when he comes to school. What happens during these years before school that has so much influence on the child's learning at later stages? We will look first at the characteristics of the way in which language develops during the period before the child starts school.

THE DEVELOPMENT OF LANGUAGE
By the age of eighteen months most normal children show that they are on the brink of using language. They now begin to associate objects and some actions with specific words and they

can produce between twelve and twenty 'words' that clearly are labels for actions or objects; they respond to familiar phrases in a way that indicates they have particular meaning. At eighteen months then the child has already taken the first step towards using language. In the next eighteen months he will master many of the features of the language he hears used by others, and by the end of his third eighteen months he will be using language in much the same way that the adults he lives with use it.

Between the ages of eighteen months and two and a half, the child not only increases the number of words that he can imitate and produce and attach meaning to, but he begins to put them together in a way that has been described as 'telegraphic' since only 'content' words are used, that is, words that represent objects and actions. The child cannot isolate the meaning of the embedding words and indeed this is not surprising. The words he can learn are those that are clearly seen to represent objects and actions. Few parents try deliberately to teach their children to use language. Most parents believe that the child's language inevitably develops just because it is characteristic of childhood. But it seems that learning to use language is, like the rest of the young child's learning, dependent on meeting appropriate experiences. Many parents talk to their young children from their earliest days almost as though they expect them to understand the meaning of what they say. In fact, what they say to the young child is always accompanied by gesture, so that meaning is demonstrated to the child through their actions and the objects they handle.

Parents intuitively repeat words and phrases so that as the child gains control of articulation he begins to imitate them. Because the child wants to communicate his wants to others he is motivated to produce those words that have come to have meaning. He puts together words that correspond to the message he wants to give, but many embedding features are missed out because he has not yet been able to isolate the meaning they carry. Parents frequently take what the child says and repeat it correctly so that the child is offered a model from which he will gradually recognize how other features are used. So the child is helped to fill out his telegraphic utterances and approaches an adult form. It is not just that the child hears language spoken and memorizes and reproduces the phrases he hears. This would **not** account for the fact that he employs particular utterances in contexts that may be very different from the contexts in which he first met them. He does not just memorize phrases, he reorders them and constructs phrases that he has never heard before. In this sense the child's utterances are original, something he has constructed for himself.

LEARNING THE RULES

The rapidity with which the child learns language is amazing, but when we think that he learns his language at a time when he cannot understand what language is, and masters complex rules of grammar at a time when explanations of grammatical rules would mean nothing to him, the learning he accomplishes appears all the more remarkable. We recognize that the child learns much about language in a very short time, but he learns it only because he is exposed to it hour after hour and day after day. The advances he makes each day may be small, but they take him surely towards mastery.

In recent years, psychologists, linguists and educationists have shown great interest in this period of development and the child's capacity for learning. Some, like Chomsky (1965) and McNeil (1970) explain this by inferring that the child has an innate capacity for knowing the rules.

The first studies of importance in the study of children's acquisition of grammatical structures were perhaps those made by Roger Brown and his associates, as they followed a two year old child round, recording all he said (Brown, Fraser and Bellugi 1970). From the analysis of the child's talk and the grammatical structures that were emerging, they were then able to forecast other structures that would appear in the child's talk, and test whether such hypothesising was sound from analysing talk recorded a little later. In this way it was possible to see that the child, even at two, was developing a simple grammar from which he operated.

McNeil has now taken this work much further and has shown that the child progresses by a series of grammars that become more complex until the grammar operated by the adults he talks with is achieved.

Thus, we have a fascinating picture emerging of the child who cannot reflect on reasons for his behaviour, who for the most part is unaware that he is using language, and who does not know what a grammar is, operating as though he were setting up and testing hypotheses about the way in which language works until he is able to extract all the grammatical rules of the language operated by adults from the talk that is going on around him.

THE DEVELOPMENT OF MEANING

Studies of this kind emphasize the way in which the child learns grammatical rules and this in itself is a fascinating study, but perhaps seem to neglect the fact that this whole development relies on the child's development of the meaning that his use of language expresses. Piaget's work has shown us that the basis for the child's developing meaning and understanding of different aspects of his experiences is the information he gains through his (Luria and Yudovitch 1959) to understand the way in which views and evidence put forward by Vygotsky (1934) and Luria sense and his actions (Piaget 1954). But we need also to note the using language in talk with adults offers the child the means by which he is drawn into the adults' way of thinking. What is said to the child alters the meaning of what he apprehends through his senses. Through the use of language by others he comes to place values on his experiences, and he comes to place them in some structure. These meanings will then underlie his thinking and will form the basis of the ideas that he will come to express as he talks with others.

There is no doubt that the young child learns to use language in a very short time, and at this very early age, but we know from our observations that all children have not learned to use language in the same way. There are differences in the meanings they have established and the thinking they express and these differences are the result of their different experiences of using language. Since the child learns to use language before he comes to school, these differences in their learning might explain differences in the way children respond to their school experiences.

SOME DIFFERENCES IN CHILDREN'S LEARNING

What do children learn to do with language by the age of three?

How do they learn to do it? What kind of differences can be found between children? How do they originate, and why should differences be regarded as important? These are important questions and were first brought to the fore more than ten years ago by Professor Bernstein and his associates at the London Institute of Education. The Bullock Report is perhaps the culmination of a growing awareness in this country that language plays an important part in children's learning and so in education. The Report urges upon teachers the need to be aware of children's developing skill in using language, since it provides not only the basis from which skills of literacy can flourish, but also a basis for all later learning. If children, for some reason, are prevented from fulfilling the potential they have for developing and using a language, then they are likely to be prevented from learning the skills and acquiring the knowledge that the teacher is trying to make available to them. Such children are without doubt at disadvantage within school. The child's disadvantage may be increased by the attitudes of teachers who do not understand the cause of the child's difficulties in school and see him as unresponsive and slow to learn.

The fact that the problem has been recognized is evident in the spread of concern to provide education in the early years for children who are at disadvantage when they come to school. Several programmes have been devised that aim to promote a development in the years before school that is more in tune with teachers' expectations and more adequate for the kinds of learning that children are faced with in school.

Thus programmes in the USA have been developed that are designed specifically to help children reach a more adequate level of language development. These programmes are generally based on helping children to acquire new linguistic structures and extend their vocabulary, particularly their knowledge of key concept words and the range of prepositions that allow more specific meaning to be expressed.

In some of these programmes there is a concentration on helping children to speak more correctly, to observe agreements, to articulate more clearly and to diminish the use of local dialect. There is a tendency to rely on instructional teaching, on drill and repetition, and to regard language as a skill to be taught in

34

isolation from the uses to which children put it. Such programmes seem to deny the role of the child's own interest, curiosity and originality in learning to use language that is seen to motivate children in the enabling home. A closer examination of what children who are at advantage in school have learned about using language in the early years and a study of the experiences at home that promote such development can provide us with insight into what our practice in school should be if the disadvantage of some children is to be redressed.

Such a piece of research was conducted by the author at the Institute of Education, the University of Leeds, between 1966 and 1972. Two groups of children, some sixty-four in all, were selected at the age of three years and were followed up at five years and at seven years of age. Half the children came from homes where parents had had the minimum period of education and earned their living at unskilled or semiskilled jobs. The remainder of the children had parents who had benefited from extended education, and one or both had proceeded to higher education and now followed professions. From the results of research we know that these groups were drawn from sections of the population which, in comparison with one another, are at advantage or disadvantage within education.

All the children were of average intelligence or above on a Stanford Binet Test at the age of three years, and as far as could be judged from visiting the home and interviewing the mother, no child was physically neglected or rejected by his parents.

When these children were three years old their language was recorded as they played with a standard set of play material and with a self-chosen playmate. These recordings lasted for at least forty-five minutes and for most of the children an hour's recording was made. Transcriptions were then made of each recording and the children's talk was then analysed in order to discover whether there were any differences in the use of language by these bright, talkative children who came from such different home environments.

The first analysis examined aspects of linguistic structure. This confirmed the findings of earlier work, for example, that of Templin (1957), Deutsch (1961) and Bernstein (1973). On all aspects of linguistic complexity, including the mean length of utterances, complexity within the noun phrases and the verb phrases, and complexity in the structure of sentences, children from the educationally disadvantaged group scored consistently less than children in the educationally advantaged group. The interesting feature was, however, that whereas in the past lower scores have been associated with lower economic status and lower intelligence, in this case the intelligence of the two groups was about the same, but there were significant differences between the groups.

Again, where in the past differences had been found at the age of five or older, differences were now found to be already well established at the age of three. On the face of it this is somewhat surprising since children at that age are so little distant from the time when they were putting together two words for intentional communication. As we have already indicated, for most children this appears to be between the age of about twenty months and two years, or two years and three months. At most this begins a year before the age of three and in many cases such behaviour may not appear until the child is two and a half or more. In our study, interviews with the children's mothers indicated that this was the case for some of the children in the study, for in little more than six months children had moved from using telegraphic utterances to a use of language that was almost adult-like. Indeed, learning is going ahead rapidly during this period for all normal children.

The differences between the groups were not in the amount of language that children had used, for although there were differences between children, there were no significant differences between the groups. Even though the children who were likely to be at educational disadvantage scored less on all measures of linguistic complexity, it was not the case that they never used the kind of complexity that characterized the language of the children who were considered to be at educational advantage. They used long utterances, extended verbs and elaborated noun phrases on some occasions. But such features occurred much less frequently than they did in the talk of children who were educationally advantaged. This was interesting since it suggested that what children had learned about language itself was not so different. Thus the children at educational disadvantage made more errors of agreement, and used a different vocabulary and articulated words differently, but still they knew a great deal about operating the language system.

This led us to consider what other aspects of children's language might be different. The crucial question seemed to be, what do children do with language? What do they use language *for*? But this is a more difficult aspect on which to make comparisons, and so far as we could discover no classification of uses of language has been developed that allows wholly objective judgments to be made and at the same time reflects anything that might be described as differences in the quality or in the complex nature of its meaning.

A classification of uses of language was established that provided a means of comparing the purposes for which children in the educationally advantaged group and those in the educationally disadvantaged group used language. Substantial differences between the groups emerged from the analysis and are summarized in the account of the work in *The Development of Meaning* (Tough 1977) as follows:

1 The disadvantaged groups of children used speech two and a half times as often as the advantaged groups to secure attention to their own needs and to maintain their own status by defending or asserting themselves in the face of the needs and actions of others.

2 The advantaged groups used language more than five times as often as the less favoured groups for extending or promoting actions, and for securing collaboration with others: language is seen to play a directing or controlling role more frequently. The disadvantage groups used language more often as part of, or as a support to, ongoing action: language tended to accompany action rather than to control or direct it.

3 The advantaged groups used language almost eight times as often to refer to past experiences and more than twice as often to contemplate the future.

4 The advantaged groups used language more than nine times as frequently for reasoning – in real or imagined contexts. The advantaged groups used more than twice as much speech for projection through the imagination as the disadvantaged

groups, and more than five times as much for projecting beyond the use of concrete materials for creating an imagined situation.

An examination of the use of language by these same children when they were at the ages of five and seven years showed that the differences that were distinguished between the groups when the children were aged three had generally increased. This was true of the complexity of structural features and for those uses of language that appear to be most relevant for the child's education. It still remained true that children in the educationally disadvantaged groups used complexity and elaboration on some occasions and that with persistent support they could produce language used for the purposes that children in the educationally advantaged group produced spontaneously.

The inferences that it seems justified to draw from this work were that it was not so much children's knowledge of language, and their inner resources of language that were different, but that they had already established very different attitudes towards the use of language, and that the purposes that they found relevant to use language for were very different.

What are the implications of these results for the education of young children? How can we ensure that all children establish a disposition to use language readily for those purposes on which their education must depend?

If we consider the way in which those children who are at educational advantage have learned to use language at home, we can perhaps gain some insight into the kind of experiences that are needed.

It is not easy to study how parents interact with their children, but it is possible through talking with mothers to gain a view of differences between them in the way in which they regard the use of language, their attitude to their children and how they are likely to use language with them, their knowledge about school and education and their attitude towards them. All these aspects seem likely to play a part in forming the experiences to which the children will be exposed in the home.

When the children were seven, their mothers were interviewed following a schedule of topics but using open questions, so that as mothers responded spontaneously, it was possible from this to gain a view of the way in which mothers interpreted the questions; the order of priorities they displayed as they answered, some reflection of the relationships they adopted towards those they spoke about, their children and neighbours and teachers; the views they held on the topics under consideration, but also an indication of the way in which they used language and the mode or modes which they adopted for organizing the information they were conveying. A full account of this work is given in *The Language of Mothers and Their Children* (Tough and Sestini (in preparation)).

It is difficult to savour the environment that surrounds a child in the home; it is a complex situation made up of material conditions and the interchange between members of the family. The child is caught up in the totality of this and each child's situation is unique. All we can do is project into the effects of certain attitudes, values, relationships towards the child and towards other people and towards the situations that impinge upon the household.

The results of this investigation confirmed much that has been indicated by other studies of interaction between mothers and their children. The most notable of these comes from Hess and Shipman (1965) and reaches the conclusion that the difference in children's learning is the result of different attitudes towards children and differences in the way in which parents talk with their children. Parents confer advantage in education on their children if they stimulate interest and curiosity, stimulate children's thinking as they talk with them, involve them in discussion about events in the past and in thinking about the future, and help them to develop problem-solving attitudes. All this comes about through the talk parents have with their children.

On the other hand, parents may use language mainly for restraining their children, and do not see that it is relevant and appropriate to explain to children the reasons for their demands. They may discourage their children from asking questions and may not involve them in planning and reflection.

The findings from studies of this kind throw some light on the kind of experiences children need if they are to develop ways of using language that are needed and expected in school. Teaching them how to use language as an end in itself is clearly not the way in which children learn to use language in the enabling home. Children learn to use language for thinking in situations where thinking is needed.

In the classroom children can most appropriately be helped to this development by the dialogue they have with the teacher about the interesting activities that have been provided.

THE IMPLICATIONS FOR CHILDREN'S LEARNING

The implications for children's learning and for the kind of experiences they ought to be offered in schools seem to be clear. The teacher needs to be aware of the kinds of skills the child has developed when he first comes to school, and working from a knowledge built up from observation and analysis should deliberately set out to involve children in experiences from which they can develop new skills and new attitudes towards the use of language.

In studying how children learn in their early years we can see that the crucial experience is the talk they have with adults about the aspects of the world that gain their attention. The nature of children's play and curiosity provides an impetus towards learning and becomes structured by the talk they have with adults from which they can develop basic concepts and attitudes of enquiry. These experiences also give the child experiences of using language in ways that can become the basis of his thinking (Tough 1973).

Crucial to this development then, is the talk that the child is having with interested and interesting adults. What goes on in the extending environment of some homes, carried out intuitively perhaps by parents, offers us a model that should be applied in schools for young children. Dialogue with a child as he plays and takes part in activities provides the meaning through which the child's thinking and use of language can be stimulated. But more than this, for as he is learning to think and communicate, he is also building concepts and skills and increasing his general stock of knowledge. Through dialogue the child can also learn to project and take the other's view, which can gradually provide the basis for the development of social responsibility and self-discipline.

How can such a policy be carried out in schools for young children? This question is discussed in a practical manner in *Listening to Children Talking* and *Talking and Learning*, two publications prepared by the Schools Council Communication Skills in Early Childhood Project, based at the University of Leeds. The view expressed is as follows: First, teachers need to understand the important role language plays in early development and in later achievement. They need to develop skills of listening to children talking and of recognizing children's need for particular language experiences as they talk with them. They need to be able to recognize the uses to which a child is putting his language and to consider how his use of language might be extended. Through the establishment of such skills teachers can engage the child in dialogue about his own activity and interests and so promote essential skills of thinking that in turn provide him with ways of interpreting his experiences that not only extend his learning but also make his time in school more meaningful and more rewarding.

BIBLIOGRAPHY
BERNSTEIN, B. (1973) *Class, Codes and Control Volume 2: Applied Studies towards a Sociology of Language* London: Routledge and Kegan Paul
BROWN, R., FRASER, C. and BELLUGI, U. (1970) 'Explorations in grammar evaluation' in R. Brown (Ed.) *Psycholinguistics* New York: The Free Press
CHOMSKY, N. (1965) *Aspects of the Theory of Syntax* Cambridge, Mass.: MIT Press
DEUTSCH, M. P. (1961) The role of social class in language development *American Journal of Orthopsychiatry* 35, 78–88
HESS, R. D. and SHIPMAN, V. (1965) Early experience and the socialization of cognitive modes in children *Child Development* 36
LURIA, A. and YUDOVITCH, F. (1959) *Speech Development and Mental Processes in the Child* London: Staples
McNEIL, D. (1970) *The Acquisition of Language* New York: Harper Rand
PIAGET, J. (1967) 'Language and thought from a genetic point of view' in D. Elkind (Ed.) *Six Psychological Studies* New York: Random House
TEMPLIN, N. C. (1957) *Certain Language Skills in Children* Oxford, England: Oxford University Press

TOUGH, J. (1976) *Listening to Children Talking: A Guide to the Appraisal of Children's Use of Language* London: Ward Lock Educational

TOUGH, J. (1977) *Talking and Learning: A Guide to Fostering Communication Skills in Nursery and Infant Schools* London: Ward Lock Educational

TOUGH, J. (1977) *The Development of Meaning* London: George Allen and Unwin

TOUGH, J. and E. SESTINI (in preparation) *The Language of Mothers and Children*

VYGOTSKY, L. S. (1934/1962) *Thought and Language* Cambridge, Mass.: MIT Press

Language development of the special child: the Miriam School

Eleanore T. Kenney

During the past four years Miriam School has participated in an outreach programme called 'The Developmental Learning Programme' (DLP) that has been carried out in the St Louis City Public School System. The DLP involves a teaching advisory network and practicum approach to help classroom teachers individualize instruction for all children. The goal is to enable increasing numbers of students with learning disorders to be identified at an early point, thus ensuring successful learning experiences in the mainstream of regular education.

The thrust of the DLP relates directly to the Bullock Committee's concern for the development of preventive measures related to reading failure; for a reappraisal of the concept of reading readiness; and for the recognition of the importance of sensory and perceptual development in relation to language development. In its present phase the DLP is funded by the Ford Foundation and managed by the Educational Confederation of St Louis. The Miriam School, as a member of the Confederation, has served as a major initial and ongoing stimulus for the evolution of the DLP philosophy.

The DLP philosophy agrees with the Bullock Committee members who do not recommend early reading as a way of enhancing language skills for most children. Such a philosophy conforms with my belief (Kenney 1976) that early reading programmes can create learning disorders for many intelligent children. As a way of elaborating on this philosophy, discussion in this paper will consider its evolution from experience gained at Miriam School through subsequent experience in the classrooms of a large public school system.

Since 1955 Miriam School has learned a great deal about children with various kinds of learning disorders. Miriam is a special day-school to help the child of normal intellectual potential who has significant learning and/or emotional disorders of such degree he is unable to achieve in regular school. (Those interested in full details regarding Miriam's preschool and primary programmes and philosophy are directed to the following references: Kenney 1964; Kenney 1969; Kenney 1971; Kenney 1976.)

Types of learning disorders – definitions and examples
Miriam's teaching philosophy represents a blend of child development and learning disability theory. It has been derived from a wide experience with many kinds of youngsters having learning disorders, many of them with serious deficits in language development. The following three general types of learning disorders of children with normal intellectual potential are defined to clarify this discussion:

Type 1 learning disorder
The child has no organically-based information processing disorder. The learning disorder is due to primary emotional disturbance or learning deprivation arising from environmental deficiencies.

Type 2 learning disorder
The child has a minor processing disorder resulting in a preferred way of learning academic skills. A learning disorder occurs due to a lack of curriculum match with the child's developmental pattern of learning.

Type 3 learning disorder – 'specific learning disability'
The child has specific and significant organically-based disorders in perceptual, integrative and/or expressive processes. Such disorders may be manifested in marked inability to listen, think, speak, read, write, spell, or do mathematical calculations.

Enrolment at Miriam includes children with all three types of learning disorders, with students aged from three to nine years. There are those Type 1 disorders that are primarily due to emotional difficulties, owing in great part to severe family problems and, possibly, pathology (i.e. the severely acting-out child; the markedly withdrawn and/or nonrelating child). In addition there are those youngsters who fit into the Type 1 category due to lack of exposure to experiences that would allow for learning to occur. These would include those children who have not been offered formal educational opportunities, as well as those with homes where there is low parental interest or neglect, or a linguistic expectation at variance with the language used in the school.

In the past, many teachers have identified most nonlearning children with normal intelligence as Type 1 learning disorders, that is, as having a primary emotional disturbance, with consequent referral for psychological or psychiatric evaluation. The goal was to remove the 'emotional block' so that the child could be emotionally free to learn. During this century, however, some educators, psychologists and physicians became increasingly aware of a group of these nonlearning children who evidence specific and significant deficits in their learning performance and yet are sensorily intact, have no primary emotional disturbance, and are intellectually normal by psychometric standards. In the early 1960s educational interest in this group of children became of such magnitude that a new area was created in special education in the United States and became known as the field of learning disabilities, giving rise to the Type 3, 'specific learning disability' category.

The Type 3 child has a major information-processing disorder that appears to be an organically based disorder within the child. Sometimes neurological irregularities are present and sometimes not. The Type 3 child evidences continuing specific disabilities in both academic and preacademic skills. Figure 1 (p. 46) presents a two-story developmental-learning model, based on Furth and Wachs (1974), that delineates preacademic and academic thinking skills. Story 1, Preacademic skills, includes the development of broad thinking skills, based in movement thinking, discriminative movement thinking, visual thinking, auditory thinking, hand graphic-thinking, logical thinking and social

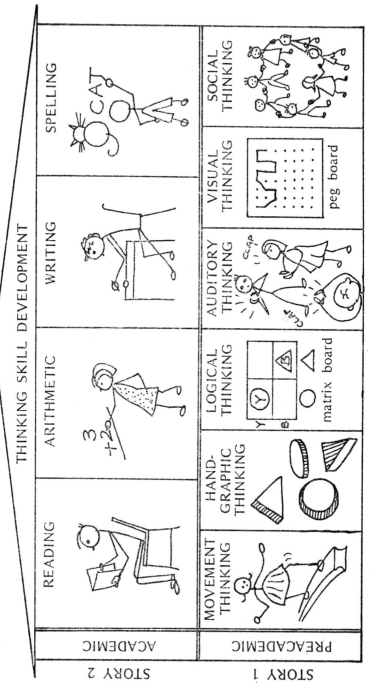

THINKING SKILL DEVELOPMENT

| STORY 2 ACADEMIC | READING | ARITHMETIC | WRITING | SPELLING |
| STORY 1 PREACADEMIC | MOVEMENT THINKING | HAND-GRAPHIC THINKING | LOGICAL THINKING | AUDITORY THINKING | VISUAL THINKING | SOCIAL THINKING |

Figure 1   Two-story developmental learning model (based on Furth and Wachs 1974)

thinking. In contrast to most children, the Type 3 child has most marked dysfunctions in the development of varied combinations of the specific processing skills at the Story 1 level. These dysfunctions make it extremely difficult for the Type 3 child to achieve certain skills at the Story 2 level of academic achievement.

The teaching of the 'hard core' Type 3 child is a challenge. It involves stating and restating, on the basis of observed behaviour, the processing dysfunctions that appear to be present, devising and redevising teaching methods whereby Story 1 and Story 2 learning skills can be developed. The ultimate teaching goal is to enable the child to compensate for the processing dysfunctions so that formal academic skills can be mastered by him. Experience at Miriam has been that the Type 3 child with major dysfunctions in verbal-expressive skills is the most difficult to help in the compensatory process, particularly with respect to the development of fluency in all aspects of language. Furthermore, we also believe that children with such verbal expressive problems should be able to be identified by no later than three years of age. The young child with normal or variable acuity in hearing, who has a significant verbal expressive deficit needs special help at as early an age as possible.

Developmental observational assessment at an early age
Given this experience with young children and the consequent belief in early idetnification, Miriam staff hold that it is highly advisable to screen for developmental dysfunctions at a much earlier age than recommended by the Bullock Committee. The Committee apparently experienced differences in opinion in this regard, with some members feeling screening should begin at the end of the infant school rather than at the beginning (17.5, p. 246). It appears to this author there was confusion by Committee members between screening for reading problems and a screen for developmental deviancies that might indicate reading problems would arise, i.e. at the reading readiness level. There was also expressed a realistic concern about the possibility of labelling a child in an inappropriate way.

We would argue that assessment on a developmental basis in relation to Story 1 skill developmental levels need not result in

47

the categorical labelling of a child. We strongly concur with the recommendations made by the Bullock Committee in sections 17.9 to 17.10 of Part Six 'Reading and language difficulties' (pp. 247–248). These relate to the importance of teacher observation as a valuable means of developmental assessment, leading to identification of strengths and weaknesses in a child's ability to learn. Mention was made of a developmental checklist that could move along with a child to help teachers know a child's best way of learning to ascertain strengths and weaknesses. The difficulty of carrying out and maintaining continuity in such a programme of developmental assessment must be noted, as it was in the Committee's Report. However, this should not deter us from seeking to carry out such a programme.

Teacher observation over time is a far more reliable source of knowledge of a child's intellectual potential than the knowledge gained from the administration of IQ tests. For too long professionals have misused individual IQ scores, with some seeming to consider them as a fixed entity in a child, never to change. Knowledge of a single IQ score actually tells us very little about a child.

An IQ score from either the Binet or Wechsler Intelligence Scale for Children represents measurements taken at a particular point in time of a number of abilities in a child, abilities such as those represented in the range of thinking skills at the Story 1 level in Figure 1. Therefore, when IQ scores are used in conjunction with teacher observation, it is important to ascertain the between and within test variability of a child's performance.

Keen teacher observation of developmental patterns should lessen the need for the extensive testing of many children. Furthermore, it should lead to the prevention of Type 2 learning disorders, i.e. the learning disorder that occurs due to a lack of curriculum match with the child's developmental pattern of learning. Such knowledge should also ensure that children are not mislabelled as having 'specific learning disabilities' when in fact it is the method of teaching that is at fault. Paragraph 18.6 (p. 268) of the section on 'Children with reading difficulties' as quoted from a group of psychologists agrees with this idea: 'If children are apparently unable to learn, we should assume that we have not yet found the right way to teach them.' This is true, particularly in the instance of the child with a Type 2 learning disorder.

Developmental teaching of the disordered child
As the Bullock Report noted, assessment of developmental deviancies is all well and good, but an answer to the following important question must also be found: What can the teacher do to help the child compensate for his particular learning disorder?

It is vital that classroom-management plans and developmentally-appropriate task demands go hand-in-hand to ensure success for the child. A basic premise is that all children, regardless of how they may appear, have a push to learn, to explore, to grow up, a wish to succeed. A general rule-of-thumb in management is the more disordered the child, the more order the teacher has to structure for that child. The freedom to be creative, to make decisions only comes when a child has developed internal self-control and a set of learning habits that make it possible for him to function independently. Children do not come to school with established learning habits. The classroom teacher is responsible for making a plan to help children develop listening skills, task-completion habits and decision-making abilities. These habits will preferably be developed in the preschool and kindergarten years. When they have not been developed at an early point it is more difficult to establish them later, particularly if the child has been continually failing many of the task demands made, such as would be true of the Type 3 specific learning disability (LD) child.

The skilled teacher has many classroom guidance techniques in her repertoire, ranging from physical management of space to expectations and shaping of varied behaviours. Clarity of teacher expectation is essential. Expectations are made known through scheduling, through giving directions verbally and visually, and through direct physical guidance when necessary. Our experience has been that much confusion in classrooms results from poorly given directions. For instance, it is frequently found that directions in teaching manuals, when precisely followed by a teacher, give too much input too fast. We all fall too readily into the trap of giving endless verbal directions, often not accompanied by visual clues. We overload children, making heavy demands on immediate memory, giving several directions at once. The LD child with processing and memory dysfunctions becomes easily overloaded on a receptive sensory basis.

In helping a child to develop a specific set of learning behaviours the teacher must believe that the child will be able to attain the goals she gets for him. This expectation by the teacher in the child is conveyed to the child in many ways. Given this expectation, there are many management techniques that can help the child achieve success. For one thing, we have found the principles and practices of behaviour modification to be valuable tools. Experience has been that these are useful ways of having the teacher become specific and perceptive about behaviours that she wants to help a child develop. Furthermore, reinforcement of positive rather than negative behaviours keeps a teacher on the alert to look for the positive and let the child know how she enjoys it. Behaviour-modification assessment is a valuable tool but, however, not a way of life.

We also often find it helpful for the teacher to talk through with the child the consequences of his behaviour in terms of self-concept, peer and adult relations. Sociometrics which help the teacher plan interaction concerned with understanding feelings, caring and sharing, are also helpful. Some youngsters and their families need more in-depth therapy and outside professional counselling to alleviate self-concept problems or family-interactional difficulties. In some instances medication has proved to be a helpful crutch, under the guidance of the child's physician. As the child comes to function independently, planned opportunities for decision-making should be initiated. It is then that the teacher sees the emergence of patterns of creative thinking channelled into useful and exciting pursuits.

As already noted, behavioural shaping must be accompanied by developmentally appropriate task demands. The teacher needs to match the curriculum demands to the child's learning profile and to the developmental level of performance that can be expected in achievement of the varied thinking skills, both preacademic and academic. This approach results in goal teaching, developmentally planned to meet the levels of sensory-motor development of the child. The teacher is knowledgeable of the individual variance in intellectual, emotional and sensory capacities, recognizing that there is a continuum of human variance in many areas of human development at all age levels.

We would argue that such developmental assessment and teaching is needed for *all* children and it is possible to carry it out in the ordinary classroom. Varied additional techniques that help include peer groupings, cross-age tutoring, and the development of learning centres to accommodate a variety of students' developmental levels of skills simultaneously.

A major endeavour at Miriam has been to help preschool, day-care and primary classroom teachers identify and alleviate developmental dysfunctions in children in their respective learning settings, preferring not to have children come to the special day-school programme that Miriam offers. To this end, an extensive community education programme has developed. Inservice workshops and practicums of varied kinds are a part of this outreach programme, with focus on imparting all aspects of the developmental assessment and teaching philosophy as set forth in this paper. A major undertaking in this area that has already been cited is the Developmental Learning Programme (DLP). The DLP is currently underway in the St Louis City Public School System. Now in its fourth year of operation, we are finding that these developmental assessment and teaching techniques can indeed be transferred to large classroom settings, with the result being that teachers devise alternative ways for individualizing management and teaching techniques to meet the learning needs of each child.

THE DEVELOPMENTAL LEARNING PROGRAMME IN THE ST LOUIS CITY SCHOOLS

The St Louis City schools have experienced all the complex problems inherent in a large urban area. In recent years it has been difficult to provide help for the classroom teachers who may have as many as thirty-five students enrolled.

The premise upon which the Developmental Learning Programme is established is that more children could be helped to be 'turned on' if the classroom teacher had available an ongoing in-system support structure that provided access to pertinent, professional growth resources. The Developmental Learning

Programme seeks to model such a structure and is composed of an advisory network, practicum training and a forum for in-school problem-solving.

Advisory network

At present the DLP operates in four subdistricts of the St Louis Public School System. Consequently there are four advisers, one in each district, relating to the staffs in schools who have chosen to take part in the programme. Initially, in the selection process, the District Superintendents polled their principals for interest and willingness to participate. Next, interested principals polled respective staffs. There are now twenty schools participating in the four districts.

Advisers are assigned to a cluster of four schools to allow for usual weekly visits. An adviser's assignment to a cluster is for up to two years. Now, in the third year of programme operation, the first adviser has shifted to another cluster of four schools within his respective subdistrict, with the same selective process obtaining (i.e. the adviser has already served for two years as an adviser to the principals and teams of teachers in four other schools in his district). As he proceeds on to help additional staffs, the adviser hopefully leaves behind four school staff that have sufficient group strength and knowhow to evolve ways to individualize instruction for all children. Hence, the advisory role is a rotating one in each district, making it possible to cover a number of schools in time and yet not add unrealistic costs to the budget of a school system.

The adviser plays a nonevaluative and helping role to class-room teachers, with a special liaison with the principal to help in developing group problem-solving meetings, described in detail below. He relates to those teachers (kindergarten to third grade) who seek his help, in their efforts to develop closer instructional matches and to create more responsive settings for children. Resulting activities with the adviser might involve the production of curriculum materials, plans for parent contacts, new ways of planning for a curriculum match in the classroom. The adviser's goal is not to make the classroom teacher dependent, but rather to lead the teacher to possible new ways of relating to children and curriculum planning.

DLP practicum training

The teaching staffs, advisers and principals in the participating schools are all required to take part in a practicum course that begins with an intensive three-day workshop before the start of the school year. It continues with weekly two-hour sessions, held after school, throughout most of the school year. The purpose of this practicum sequence is to extend knowledge and competence in all of the areas outlined in this paper under the DLP philosophy. In particular, the practicum seeks to help classroom teachers to become keen observers and to enrich their instructional repertoires, at the same time matching the curriculum to individual learning needs.

The practicum employs a case-study approach with each teacher selecting a single child of concern and developing a means of assessing the child developmentally with respect to all Story 1 skills. We find that observing skills are enhanced and teachers begin to understand better the behaviours and learning profiles of other children in their classrooms. Teacher expectations about particular children change, and they frequently put ideas into action in the classroom shortly after discussion has occurred in the course. This approach seems to answer many of the concerns reflected in the Bullock Report that related to re-training classroom teachers in a way that allows them to put theory into practice. Integral in the practicum format is the discussion method, affording ongoing problem-stating and problem-solving experiences for the teaching staffs at each school.

The principals' participation in the practicum training has proved to be of inestimable value both to the principals and to the teachers, yielding as it does ongoing communication about management and curriculum plans that are developing. Principals have expressed the belief that their participation gave them greater awareness of the primary curriculum and enabled them to gain real insight into the learning process in classrooms. They have also been better able to assess the quality of teaching that is occurring, helping them in their own evaluation of each teacher. Teachers have confirmed this in expressing increased confidence that their principals could now evaluate their performance with greater understanding and sensitivity.

In-school problem solving

The development of regular team meetings in each school is an important part of the DLP. Meetings are convened by the principal who, together with the adviser, plans the format. All participating staff take part in the meetings, which are also open to other school staff and parents as well. Initially, the most useful format for a meeting has proved to be the 'staffing' of one of the children that has been identified as a teacher's case study. The teacher and ancillary personnel concerned with the child participate in stating the child's learning or behaviour problems. Subsequently, the entire group joins in to suggest ways of dealing with the problem, both in the classroom and in the school.

An important member of the team is the Educational Resource Teacher (ERT), a school-based person charged with the responsibility of helping a caseload of twenty children who have difficulty in learning basic skills. This teacher's role had previously been based on a 'pull out' model, with classroom teachers referring children to work with him individually or in small groups. He was seen as a 'special education' teacher who really had nothing to do with what happened in the classroom. The DLP seeks to help him change this image and become a true resource to the classroom teacher, addressing the help he gives children to difficulties experienced in the classroom.

In some instances it may be the ERT will move in and work with particular children in groups in the classroom. His diagnostic knowledge of the child adds valuable information to the team meetings. In many instances he has played a major role in preparing format for team meetings. He serves as a valuable in-school person to help the adviser in developing school-staff communication. Experience has indicated that the adviser-ERT combination has gone far in helping the classroom teacher meet the wide range of individual differences in each room.

The Bullock Report noted patterns of different remedial help. Apparently in Great Britain, 'The part-time teacher and the class teacher often work independently, and few schools have a member of the staff with special responsibility for coordinating the work and advising' (p. 272, 18.16). In the United States the recent push for 'mainstreaming' of more children with special problems has necessitated the development of improved ways to keep children in the normal classroom, at the same time serving their needs. The slowly emerging role of the ERT in the DLP programme gives promise of being able to achieve much in this regard.

Thus it is that the Developmental Learning Programme has evolved, with beginnings in experience gained in special education at Miriam School, leading to this current programme that is carried out in classrooms in the St Louis City schools.

CONCLUSIONS

As stated at the outset of this article, this author proposes that this Developmental Learning Programme (DLP) furnishes something of an answer to the Bullock Committee's concerns for the development of preventive measures related to reading failure; the reappraisal of the concept of reading readiness; the recognition of the importance of sensory and perceptual development in relation to language development. Furthermore, it is proposed that the DLP is a direct answer to the issue raised by the Bullock Committee in the chapter on 'Children with reading difficulties' (18.19, p. 275):

> Preventive measures are likely to be far more productive than remedial ones ... a very great deal can be done to prevent reading disability by raising the quality of teaching generally and by giving skilled individual help before a sense of failure has led the child to lose confidence.

The DLP, with its practicum and staff-development components, most certainly does offer a way to improve the quality of teaching in normal classrooms. In addition, it ensures that classroom teachers are knowledgeable of the individual variance in intellectual, emotional and sensory capacities, recognizing that there is a continuum of human variance in many areas of human development, at all age levels. This approach leads to goal teaching, developmentally planned to meet the levels of sensory-motor development of each child, ensuring the optimum environment for language development for all children.

REFERENCES

FURTH, H. G. and WACHS, H. (1974) *Thinking Goes to School* New York: Oxford University Press

KENNEY, E. T. (1964) 'The small classroom – a–development idiosyncratic approach to learning and behavioural disorders in children with normal intelligence' in *Inspection and Introspection of Special Education* Council for Exceptional Children

KENNEY, E. T. (1969) 'A diagnostic preschool for atypical children' in 'Out of the Classroom' *Exceptional Child* 36, 193, November

KENNEY, E. T. (1971) 'Education for children with learning disabilities' in Jack Hartstein (Ed.) *Current Concepts of Dyslexia* St Louis: Mosby and Co

KENNEY, E. T. (1975) Learning disability: what it is and is not *Educational Leadership*, May

KENNEY, E. T. (1971) 'Education for children with learning disabilities' mental Teaching of Children with Learning Disorders. Talk given at Conference on Learning Disorders, jointly sponsored by the Council for Exceptional Children and the Association for Children with Learning Disabilities and the Alabama Chapter of the American Academy of Pediatrics. Mobile, Alabama, May

3   Language across the curriculum

INTRODUCTION
Each article in this section calls attention to important aspects of language in the school setting, particularly to the attitudes that we and our students have towards it. In this regard, all the articles point us away from a concern with correctness and propriety in form and mechanics, away from the current 'back to basics' concern with rightness or wrongness in the surface features of language. As these authors suggest, there is much more to language than that, especially when we give serious consideration to questions about the relationship of language to thinking and to learning.

Mike Torbe offers a critique of the image of the teacher as 'moral guardian' of language, as well as a description of the view of learning implied by this position. He then provides a picture of the teacher who has a very different view of language, and thus of learning. To make this alternate picture more concrete, he includes several examples of classroom language drawn from his own experience.

Bryan Newton turns our attention from teachers to students. He describes how the student's view of himself as a learner affects his school performance. Drawing on the insights of George Herbert Mead and the speech and writing of students, Newton discusses the process by which students internalize a set of attitudes towards their own language in relation to the language of school. Students, he says, want to participate more actively in their own learning, especially through the medium of their language. Teachers' attitudes towards language and learning, though, must change dramatically before this can occur.

Moving back to teachers once again, Robert Parker describes how this dramatic change in attitudes towards language and learning that Newton calls for might take place. Through writing themselves, for their own purposes, and discussing their writing with others, teachers can explore the writing process from the 'inside'. In this way, as the excerpts he presents from teachers' journals demonstrate, they learn more about why we write, how writing happens, and the ways in which writing can best serve our purposes for growth and learning.

Each writer calls for a more open, flexible classroom – one in which the intentions of both students and teachers can be more fully and fruitfully realized through language.

The secret-sharers: teachers' response to language across the curriculum

Mike Torbe

Despite the long history of language study, many of the most widely-held ideas about language are either superficial or false. It is widely believed that language is 'communication', that we learn it by imitating and copying, and that we speak in words and sentences. Above all, there is the feeling that language standards are progressively declining, because people talk lazily and carelessly, and write inaccurately, ignoring the rules of grammar and logic. Such ideas are not just false notions about language, but also indicate a whole range of submerged and mysterious attitudes to society as well.

These attitudes also shape the teaching of the many teachers who share them. Language is seen as 'communication', mainly by the teacher to the pupil, and the pupil is expected to 'communicate back' what he has heard, and to say clearly what he means. Because language is learned by imitation and copying, pupils can extend and improve their language by copying and imitating the teacher or the textbook. Because we speak in words and sentences, pupils are encouraged to 'finish words properly', and to 'talk in complete sentences'. For these teachers, language has two main functions: it indicates that the pupil has accepted the necessary demands education makes, and it represents the medium in which knowledge is transmitted and displayed.

The ways in which a teacher deals with the surface conventions of language offer important clues to his submerged attitudes. The teacher who said, 'I've told them they'll only get an A for their work if it's very neat' was taking up a moral stance to a strictly nonmoral matter. By applying criteria normally associated with desirable social behaviour of a particular kind, she was demonstrating that she was concerned more, apparently, with linguistic etiquette than with intellectual performance.

When the features of the language that is demanded are expected to suit ideas of what is proper, rather than what is effective, then the teacher is apparently seeing himself not only as a teacher, but also as guardian of a social and moral code, dealing with children who are ignorant of the code, and whose ignorance is confirmed by their ignorance also of the linguistic conventions that go with it. Beginning sentences with 'and' or 'but'; ending sentences with prepositions; leaving out main verbs (and then not knowing what a main verb is): these things cause offence well out of proportion to the apparent fault. A research study (Briggs 1970) which showed that children with untidy handwriting are assessed by teachers as being of lower ability than pupils with neat handwriting, irrespective of the content of the writing, comes as no surprise. Tidiness and accuracy are next to perfection, and indicators of a desirable moral code. Language etiquette is equated with moral fibre.

This notion of the teacher as moral guardian goes very deep. For example, although in some subjects of the curriculum, errors in language conventions apparently cause less offence than others, there is a curious double-think involved. The science teacher who 'marks for the science', or the history teacher who 'looks for the facts', appear not to be concerned with linguistic conventions; but they may be ready to point to pupils' inability to spell or punctuate as evidence of the moral decline of the nation. For academic success in a subject, it is knowledge that is looked for; language is not thought of as important, except when errors suggest a refusal or inability by the pupil to accept the social and linguistic norms expected by the subject teacher.

These attitudes to language bring with them inevitable attitudes to learning. Even though the connection may not be explicitly recognized, all teachers know intuitively that there is some relationship between language and learning. It is expressed normally in terms of the public face of language as communication, in which what has been learned can be publicly displayed, as essay or lecture for instance, rather than in terms of the processes by which learning has itself occurred. When it is the publicness of the statement that is being stressed, then inevitably what is important is that the language should be publicly acceptable and not offend the listener or reader.

But defining language as public communication may make it difficult to see that most classroom learning involves pupils in beginning to understand new ideas, rather than making public statements; and since the language in which new understanding is first expressed is rarely well-organized, carefully formulated or polished, the teacher whose definition stresses proper public language may reject or at least undervalue it. When the language is undervalued, the learning that can only go on in that kind of language is undervalued, too; thus, the teacher who has powerful feelings about social standards and norms probably has corresponding beliefs about learning which stress the public organization of knowledge. Being a subject-specialist, then, means seeing the subject as a microcosm of society and as a kind of speech-community; entering the subject means acquiring and using the language which comes with it. The scientist and the historian do not pay attention to language, because they do not separate it in any way from the knowledge itself. The only time they do become conscious of it is when it intrudes itself by being socially inappropriate in terms of the society of the subject, as, for instance, when a historical essay is written in such a way as to disturb ideas of acceptable linguistic behaviour.

That these hypotheses about the social and moral, as well as intellectual aspects of curriculum thinking have some basis is supported by traditional beliefs about the varying moral effects of learning different things. The product of a Latin degree has, it is believed, a totally dissimilar mind to a scientist or historian, not because a different personality or set of interests led him to choose one subject or another, but because studying Latin has *made* him different. And there have been strong notions of the moral reverberations of studying one subject rather than another: the conventional image of the scientist, according to a recent survey,[1] is that he is cautious, calm, realistic, atheistic and would not necessarily 'stop work if he thought it was harmful'. This may be compared with ideas about the values, largely moral, of studying literature.[2]

The model of teaching and learning which lies behind the attitudes described so far can be characterized as one which stresses transmission of knowledge from one generation to another. It asserts that the teacher-pupil relationships needed for that transmission symbolize the necessary authority relationship of society itself, and creates a formal institutional structure that legitimates and defends that authority. Deviant or personal utterances may be seen as challenges to the structure, because it has no means of assessing their value. The model emphasizes the public product rather than the process that generates it, because the process is apparently private, the preserve of the individual; and the product is expected to conform to established canons of taste and appropriacy.

This 'transmission' model (to use Douglas Barnes's (1974) term) is only one: others are possible, which present very different beliefs about language and learning, and thus about curriculum. Not public only then but personal; not product only but process; not knowledge only but learning. The teacher's role as moral guardian is exchanged for a totally different role, of careful, attentive, sensitive listener or reader, who feeds back to the student an image of himself as a learner. He believes that the student comes to him not ignorant but knowing – but knowing and valuing different things about the teacher. He believes that public language is important, but that it should come at a later stage. New information and ideas have to be taken in and understood before the learner can write or talk in a polished, confident, formal way about them. The process of coming to terms with new learning is tentative and hesitant, and to demand an immediate move to public language without helping the learner to use his language to make his own understandings is to leave out the crucial learning process. There are always several stages before a learner is ready for public communication, so this teacher's road to public language is very different from the 'transmission' teacher's. The teacher who begins from talk, who recognizes the differences between talk and writing, and who has insights into the ways language and learning operate, is prepared to accept kinds of talking and writing that the other teacher probably rejects as careless, unformed, untidy or useless. He accepts them because he sees them not as something irrelevant, to be rigorously excluded, but as evidence of first-draft learning, where the child is beginning to come to terms with new ideas and feelings. Talk which is hesitant, unpredictable and anecdotal, writing which is free-wheeling and half-formulated, are as important to him, therefore, as more polished, formulated work, because they are the necessary ways in which a pupil moves toward public language.

A necessary part of *all* teachers' work is considering the relationship between language and learning. One way of doing this is by redrawing the map of the classroom and its language events, and entering into negotiation with events and people in the classroom, recognizing what is new about situations previously thought of as familiar. Let me explain what I mean through three examples. The first is a matter of practical definition, the second an analysis of a familiar context, and the third, the way teachers have controlled the language-and-learning theory and brought it into the classroom.

The definition first. When I was at school, what I hated and feared most in English was the precis. I was consistently unable to understand the passages set, or to 'reduce to one-third of the length', or, above all, to put it 'in my own words'. When I started teaching English, it was precis that I found most difficult to teach, and that my pupils, no doubt, found most unpleasant. Now, in my professional life, what skill do I use and value above all? Why, the precis. If I have to teach it now, I begin from a totally different definition of what it is about: I no longer see it as a game with words, whose rules I do not know, nor as a publicly demanded mode of language, with particular social requirements. Instead, I begin from the question of purpose and process, and redefine precis as the process by which a reader understands in his own terms a passage which he is reading for specific purposes. Precis is thus not about words, but about *ideas*. Such a redefinition aims to place in the pupils' hands the underlying intentions of the work they do, rather than simply demanding obedient acceptance of a purposeless task. Moreover, by exploring jointly the process of understanding a piece of reading, it is possible to see the fundamental purposes of precis and note-taking as powerful ways of capturing and controlling meaning, whatever subject of the curriculum is being explored. Such an exploration can come naturally as part of a belief about language and learning.

Secondly, here is a brief snatch of familiar classroom talk. Three thirteen year old boys are doing a scientific experiment in which the heating of an iron bar causes a pointer (a bent needle, on which the bar is resting) to register the expansion of the bar. An adult visitor is with them.

(Italic type means that two people are talking simultaneously. (?) means the speech is not transcribable.)

1 Visitor: See what's happening to the needle?
2 Boy 1: Yes, it's going down
3 Boy 2: Yes, I know
4 Visitor: Why is it doing that?
5 Boy 1: Best part will be (?)
6 Boy 2: Because Ian's knocking it
7 Boy 1: No it isn't it –
8 Boy 3: Yes it is because I was knocking the chair then and it was going down
9 Visitor: Well no one's knocking it now, look.
   (The needle is still moving)
10 Boy 1: No
11 Boy 3: Yes well that – the erm – the heat molecules are pushing the –
12 Boy 1: No they're not
13 Boy 3: Well anyway *that thing's going down*
14 Boy 1: *They're expanding*
15 Visitor: What's expanding?
16 Boy 1: The er – heat molecules are giving more energy, *so they need more room* to move about and so the bar has to get longer so it goes down, the needle
17 Boy 3: (?) *that thing's going down it's got something to do with that.* Oh yes because when the bar goes longer it *the thing pushes that thing down and makes that* go down. Yes because it that's that, it turns it round, and that goes down
18 Boy 1: *Yes, pushes that out, makes that go out*

This is the stuff of learning: pupils negotiating with each other about the meaning of what they are experiencing. At (6) the boy gives an utterly pragmatic explanation in terms of his past experience. The specific context of science is less important to him than the existing patterns of meaning in his head which create his own expectations: things move like that because someone touches or knocks them. Boy 1 (7) contradicts, but without having the chance to explain why, because at (8) the other boy also supports the 'commonsense' explanation. If the three boys had been alone, the two might have defeated the one, simply by the pressure of two refusing to admit the objection of one; but the adult acts as midwife to learning, not by commenting directly on the argument, but by directing attention again to what is actually happening at (9). Boy 3 is forced to reconsider, and draws now on a half-recollection of what the teacher has previously taught the class about the reason for the pointer's moving (11). Although his formulation is closer now to what the objector might accept, Boy 1 feels it is inaccurate in its understanding, and takes up the explanation. It is both an inwards- and outwards-directed formulation: he is explaining to the adult ('communicating') but is also testing out his own understanding ('learning'). At (12), (14) and (16) he shows that he has not just remembered but is at least on the way to *understanding* the theory as explained by the teacher. During his utterance at (16), Boy 1 moves further towards tentativeness (the first line of 17) and then triggered, by his friend, makes a leap of learning, signalled by his own formulation, which is both acceptance and extension of what his friend has said: 'Oh yes . . .' His friend supports him with a slight reformulation of Boy 3's utterance at (18), which Boy 3 accepts – 'yes . . .'

Two central points to note: one is that without the adult's two comments at (4) and (9), and perhaps his request for extension at (15), it's possible the boys would not have verbalized their understanding, or talked of it at all. The second point is that they learn by talking. By 'learning' here, I mean finding out for themselves what they understand or don't, testing out new thinking on other people, and verbalizing it so they can inspect the implications of their utterances. I think this snippet of discussion marks a growth point; although they by no means fully understand molecular theory, they are further down the road towards understanding than they were before, not just because they have done the experiment, but because they have been forced by the situation to talk about it. Without the talk, the ideas and understanding would have remained latent and inchoate. Believing in the crossover relationship between language and learning means that the teacher has not only to tolerate this kind of talk, but to encourage it, holding back if necessary the approved language of the subject. Indeed, it is quite possible, as all teachers know, for pupils to be able to reproduce teacher or book language perfectly, without in any way understanding what they are saying or writing. Here, the boys are discovering that they can talk their way in to understanding, even though they are not yet ready to explore molecular theory formally.

The third example is an inevitable extension of the second. Once the teacher does become conscious of the way language and learning interact, then he can place the processes of learning in the hands of the pupils. Not only by explaining to them the public demand of precis, essay or science learning, but by making them conscious of the underlying processes, he gives his pupils a power over their own learning which has enormous consequences not only for education, but for the lives they will lead. One teacher,[3] for instance, gave his pupils advice on 'How to do projects'. The advice is intensely practical, and following it would clearly produce better project work in the secondary school; but it also explains for the pupils, a fundamental theory about writing:

These suggestions are for the purpose of making projects more useful. To follow them, you need to understand something about different sorts of writing.

1   Books are written to be read by anybody. That's why they're written the way they are. The man writing the book doesn't know who's going to read it or where or when. The audience he's addressing is the public. And he's addressing them for a very clear purpose – to tell them things he thinks they'll want to know.

2   You know more or less who your readers are going to be – your tutors, maybe some other people in your year, an assessor. When you're writing to someone you know you don't write the way book-writers do. You know you can just be yourself and you don't pretend the whole world is going to read your words. Think of the writing you do in your logbooks, those of you that use the log as a way of

talking to your tutor. Some of the best writing that gets done is in log books – because it's honest and relaxed.

3 Sometimes you only write for yourself. That's a different sort of writing again. Say you are making notes on a book, and you know the only person those notes will be useful to is you, later. You won't need to spell everything out, you can use symbols and abbreviations and shorthand. This is writing for an audience of yourself.

Another teacher[4] explained to his secondary school pupils 'How your English work will be marked', with the comment, 'if your parents take an interest in your English and read your work, let them read this too'. Here again, the teacher makes explicit to the pupils underlying principles which are not normally displayed:

When your teachers do choose to mark your work, it may not always be to correct or grade it (though they may keep grades, which they do not write on your work, in their mark books, to record your progress). How it is marked depends on what your work is intended to be and who it is intended for. If you tell your teacher, someone you know, about something interesting, you should expect him to reply in the same way, like a pen-friend. If you are trying out a way of writing on the teacher, you'd expect to receive help on how to write that way, like a master's advice to an apprentice. If you've written to prove your competence at something – a test – expect to be told how far you've succeeded (a grade) and where you've gone wrong (correction) . . .

These approaches are subversive, and what they subvert is the notion of education as a closed, mysterious, hierarchical activity. They demystify teaching by opening up to pupils and their parents control over their own learning and offering a cooperative endeavour with a common purpose, that the pupils should become autonomous learners. Such a definition of learning is subversive of existing curricula and teaching styles because it asserts above all the vitality of the student's own language as the central way in to learning, and therefore to successful public language. It is open, where the other model is closed.

I have suggested that moralistic attitudes to language are no accident, that what appear to be purely linguistic opinions are connected with far more complex and inexplicit ideas which reject the intrinsic relationship between language and learning in education. The attitudes to language and learning, then, are political attitudes, but it is a politics which is deeply embedded in the inscape of individuals and groups. The complex of beliefs about authority and its moral dues; about obedience to external criteria accepted as given; about paying due regard to a heritage of experience, whether or not such regard is justified: these and other beliefs help to map out a political stance. The stance itself originates, it seems, in the interaction between the objective and historical reality of political parties and their philosophies, and the particular psychological and social history of the individual, who finds that a political philosophy expresses his own inexpressible intuitions about people, life and relationships. Those who sustain ideas about language which the mildest documentation would show to be untrue, or reject ideas which are demonstrably accurate, are saying something about their image of themselves and their place in the world. A teacher is a professional dealing with professional matters, and gaining his professional identity from that: mathematics and history and science are school subjects and part of a professional preserve. But the way people talk to each other and allow others to talk to them is not a professional mystery but public property. A teacher who begins to see that language is the core of learning and therefore of the entire educational process is forced to recognize that learning does not only occur because he causes it to. He is faced with a disturbing mirror of himself in his own language encounters with pupils, friends, family and strangers. Sometimes, this is too much to face: people's fears about language and how others use it, reflect back to them their own fears about their inadequacies as people.

Schools have chosen to face the questions about language and learning that the Bullock Report has raised because they are part of a greater movement in a culture. It is not that the past is being rejected, that morality itself is under attack, or that 'language across the curriculum' is destructive of existing good. On the contrary, it is regenerative: it breathes life into dusty ideas and draws to it all the old powerful concepts of the school as a community. Now, though, it is a genuine community that is being sought, one which crosses subject boundaries and holds together intellectually as well as socially, not by external compulsion, but by an inner coherence and a shared identity and purpose.

REFERENCES

BARNES, D. and SHEMILT, D. (1974) Transmission and interpretation *Educational Review* 26,3

BRIGGS, D. (1970) The influence of handwriting on assessment *Educational Research* 13,1

NOTES

1 The survey was jointly conducted by *New Society* and *New Scientist*, August 28, 1975.
2 See especially the work of F. R. Leavis, Denys Thompson, and Fred Inglis.
3 Peter Medway, Head of Faculty, Crofton High School, Wakefield, Yorkshire.
4 Andrew Stibbs, Head of Faculty, English Department, Brotton High School, Clevelan.

The learner's view of himself

Bryan Newton

'But if you please, Miss Louisa,' Sissy pleaded, 'I am – oh so
stupid!'

Louisa, with a brighter laugh than usual, told her she would
be wiser by-and-by.

'You don't know,' said Sissy, half crying, 'what a stupid girl
I am. All through school hours I make mistakes. Mr and Mrs
M'Choakumchild call me up, over and over again, regularly to
make mistakes.'

'Mr and Mrs M'Choakumchild never make mistakes themselves, I suppose, Sissy?'

'Oh no!' she eagerly returned. 'They know everything.'
(Charles Dickens *Hard Times* , 1854)

'. . . if it's contrary to what the book says, then you think you're
wrong. I don't know why, but you do – you tend to think of
the critics as always being right. I always think of the teacher
as always being right . . . you think because they're a teacher
they've got their English and they're bound to be right.'
(Nobby, sixth-form comprehensive school pupil, 1975)[1]

'Plus ça change . . .' It's clear that Sissy Jupe has an unequivocal
view of her abilities as a learner – 'I am – oh so stupid'. Nobby,
while less certain of his stupidity, is painfully aware of his inadequacies: 'I'd like to write in a nice style so that everybody
could understand it but I can't find that possible.'

So, just as Sissy Jupe couldn't produce the required definition of a horse, so Nobby can't find the writing style that is
acceptable to his teachers. The effect of this on Nobby's view
of himself as a learner was expressed through his comments upon
his teachers:

I suppose yon think them to be more intelligent, so you try and, you know, catch up with them I suppose – try and be equal – and you know it's not possible so you don't want to say anything . . . they've influenced me, I don't think I could think for myself.

Nobby is not an exceptional case. Many pupils hold similar views of themselves as learners and writers within the school context. I want to suggest some of the reasons for the feelings of inadequacy experienced by pupils in school, to look at their suggestions for change and at a situation in which change seems to have taken place.

The view of ourselves which we hold is socially determined and as a school exhibits many of the characteristics of a total institution[2] it sets up its own 'organized social process of experience and behaviour'. That phrase comes from George Herbert Mead, who in *Mind, Self and Society* (Mead 1934) offers an analysis of the social genesis of the self which may be helpful in enabling us to understand the way that children's views of their own abilities develop and are reinforced within the school context.

Having reached the conclusion that 'it is impossible to conceive of a self arising outside of social experience', Mead then develops the concept of the self as consisting of two parts – the 'I' and the 'me'.

The 'I' is the response of the organism to the attitudes of others; the 'me' is the organized set of attitudes of others which one himself assumes. The attitudes of the others constitute the organized 'me', and then one reacts to that as an 'I'.

If Mead is right, the child internalizes the attitudes of the school and its teachers, creating an organized school 'me', which he then responds to. We may think of it as a dialogue between the two parts of the self ('So I said to myself . . .') in which the 'I' is trying (or sometimes not trying) to measure up to the 'me's' standards.

Mead makes the point thus in terms of the individual's behaviour in relation to society:

. . . social control, as operating in terms of self-criticism, exerts itself so intimately and extensively over individual behaviour or conduct, serving to integrate the individual and his actions with reference to the organized social process of experience and behaviour in which he is implicated. . . . That is to say, self-criticism is essentially social criticism, and behaviour controlled by self-criticism is essentially behaviour controlled socially.

So, within school, the 'me' of the child's self is largely 'the organized set of attitudes' of teachers and of the school and it is from these attitudes that the child's self-criticism derives its substance – and thus his view of himself as a learner.

Look at the following bit of conversation with a thirteen year old girl:

BN: You said you weren't very good at writing poems, didn't you?

Sandra: No, I'm not very good at it.

BN: Now why do you say that?

Sandra: Because when I was at primary school I got a very low mark for a poem that I'd done and the teacher put underneath it: poetry isn't your bright spark, or something, is it? And that's what put me off, I think.

Notice that Sandra doesn't say that one teacher didn't think much of a poem she wrote. What she says is 'I'm not very good at it'. For her, the school 'me' is also the personal 'I'.

We can see a similar generalizing process in the following comment from an eleven year old:

Jeannette: Well, it mostly fairly tales I write about, because Mr A always commented I've got a good imagination for fairy tales, so I'm about pixies and fairies and goblins and things.

Mr A was Jeannette's primary-school teacher. She was in a secondary school when she made that comment.

It is apparent from talking to children that their primary-school experience – where they have one teacher for most of their lesson time in any one year – can leave a very strong impression on them. It is, apparently, very difficult for some children to respond to the school 'me', to their teachers' views of them as learners, by rejecting or being critical of these views. They are what their teachers say they are. In the secondary school, where they normally have different teachers for every subject, they tend to become more aware of the variety of expectations which their teachers have for them. While this does not necessarily effect a marked change in their view of themselves as school learners, it does sometimes make them more aware of the games they are being expected to play:

At secondary school it was always writing to please whichever teacher was taking you.
(Third-year college student)

A fifteen year old boy, Steve, said:

To be honest I would try and make something suit a particular person that I was writing for – I wouldn't change my opinions for that person, probably not consciously, but when I look back at things I find they're different when they're for different teachers, although I didn't intentionally make them different. Um – yeah – put different things in a different sort of framework that would suit the teacher.

Nobby, the sixth-form pupil I quoted earlier, finds this kind of accommodation to his teachers' expectations more difficult:

I start an essay or something and I think 'I've gone wrong here' and I have to start again – I'm always thinking of writing in their style. . . . You're thinking so much of writing in their style that you're not really thinking what you're writing about.

Pupils, then, quickly internalize a model of what the teacher wants. In some cases they will strive to provide it (especially younger children). A ten year old writing about writing:

If it is not good I feel bad in some ways if it is good work I feel paids (pleased) with myself. Becames the thether will be happ and then I will be happ becames I want the thether to be happ.

In other cases there is a cynical provision of what the teacher wants. Recollecting her experience of school writing, a teacher (not a teacher of English) described writing 'a most revoltingly flowery piece of prose' which was warmly praised by her teacher. She concluded:

> ... from then on it was easy – if that was what they wanted that was what they were going to get. From henceforth large quantities of drivel flowed from my pen to be greeted with continuous approbation. For me, honest creative writing was dead.

When we reflect upon the power of teachers, we can see why so many children try so hard to please them. They are often the only assessor of the pupils' work – and the work arises from situations they set up. There is thus the danger, even with the best-intentioned teacher, of a distorting influence being constantly at work upon the child's learning processes. The internalized 'other' will not allow sufficient space for the child to develop his own strategies for learning or his own paths for growing.

If we add to this the stress placed by many schools on writing as a means of testing that learning has taken place, the frequent insistence on 'appropriate' language (usually the language of the subject), the frequent remoteness of the subject matter from the child's own experience, the competitive nature of many learning situations, the lack of opportunities for undirected talk, then we have a situation where it might seem that obstacles were being deliberately placed in the way of learning.[3]

Awareness of obstacles to learning is implicit (and sometimes explicit) in the view expressed by some fifteen year old pupils who were invited to write about 'the importance of language in education' by their geography teacher.[4] The comments they made showed both the influence of school models and an awareness of the limitations of these models. For instance, one comment which suggested an acceptance of the school view was:

In order to increase your vocabulary you must increase your knowledge, and you only receive the new knowledge at school, where you are educated. . . . Education is where your teacher explains certain facts to you.
(Paul)

Another comment suggested an awareness of the boundaries of school 'learning' – but still seems to imply acceptance of the validity of it:

To me education is very important. We never stop learning things all the time we have experiences, experience is learning. So, we can be educated by our senses, we remember our experiences and feelings. This broadens our outlook on life and is very important because it helps us to appreciate the quality of life. The other type of education is what basically we learn in school, that is factual events, etc. These give us satisfaction in knowing them and we can be tested *exactly* to see what we know.
(David)

Notice the split between affective and cognitive in that comment. School learning is perceived as low-level cognitive – facts to be tested for. What is most striking here is that David is not complaining; he seems well disposed towards school. He is simply reflecting the nature of the situation as he sees it.[5]

This separation between 'experience' and 'facts' is the subject of a telling paragraph in the Bullock Report:

It is a confusion of everyday thought that we tend to regard 'knowledge' as something that exists independently of some-one who knows. 'What is known' must in fact be brought to life afresh within every 'knower' by his own efforts. . . . In order to accept what is offered when we are told something, we have to have somewhere to put it; and having somewhere to put it means that the framework of past knowledge and experience into which it must fit is adequate as a means of interpreting and apprehending it. Something approximating to 'finding out for ourselves' needs therefore to take place if we are to be successfully told. The development of this individual context for a new piece of information, the forging of the links that give it meaning is a task we customarily tackle by talking to other people. (p. 50)

If we accept this view from Bullock, that we must recreate knowledge for ourselves in our own terms and with our own language, then we must question, as Deborah does in the following passage, the narrow range of language use promoted by schools.

In school you do not have to use language to express your opinions a great deal. When you do have to express your opinions it is usually in written form and so you do not gain much experience of actually talking and expressing your opinions to someone else. I think we should have time in school for discussing various topics. As well as gaining knowledge by listening to others, we would also learn to inform others of our knowledge and opinions.
(Deborah)

Consider also the force of this comment, where the difficulty of being obliged to use other people's language is seen clearly as an obstacle to understanding:

I find that when a teacher dictates notes, they are much harder to understand than a teacher who does not. As he or she, whatever the case may be, has their own way of writing the information, and sometimes it can be somewhat of a problem to understand the notes given. Whereas a teacher who does not use this method, and will only explain what is to be said I find is much more easily understood, as when you come to write up the notes, you can write what you think and not what someone else has told you.

By using this method, I find one can adapt whatever ability one has in English, to rewriting the notes, using one's knowledge. In a way that they can be understood.
(Royston)

Many of the pieces of writing which these students composed pointed to their desire to participate more actively in the learning process rather than just remaining as passive recipients of teacher and book knowledge. The 'I' of each of these pupils has begun to respond critically to the passive, fact-oriented, put down the notes and give them back on the test 'me' that their teachers have been telling them is the best way to be a school learner. They are beginning to know better, to realize that their teachers may have been selling them a social bill of goods; but they have little confidence and less power so they will be able to do very little about their growing awareness.

Of course pupils' views of themselves as learners are not derived wholly from their experience in school. Their homes and other social contexts in which they find themselves may provide other views – which is why they may come to reject what the school offers or why, as they mature as learners, they may recognize the serious limitations of what the school often promotes as 'learning'. Nevertheless schools have immense influence in determining what kind of confidence pupils have in their own abilities.

We are surely now in a position to do something to remove many of the impediments which schools may place in the way of their pupils' learning. The Schools Council Project *The Development of Writing Abilities 11–18* (Britton 1975) directed by Professor James Britton formulated two useful concepts for identifying the kinds of writing that pupils do in school – the concepts of 'function' and 'audience'; that is, what purpose the writing is serving and who the writer has in mind as his reader(s). The research team found in their sample that the bulk of school writing was for the restatement of information in much the same terms that the teacher of the textbook had given it out in the first place and that the audience for the writing was usually the teacher perceived by the writer as an 'examiner' – that is, someone who would assess and correct something that he already knew. The conclusion of the research team was that pupils' opportunities for learning through writing were very limited in schools—that the range of options in terms of functions and audience started narrow (at age eleven) and became narrower as the pupils became older. The research team's view, naturally enough, was that there should be a wide range of options open to pupils – and they laid particular stress on the importance of writing where pupils could express a response to information they were dealing with: where the 'I' to 'me' response relationship could in fact be encouraged to function.

So, as we are concerned here with the pupil's view of himself as a learner within the school context we can see a number of reasons why the model of successful learning presented by the school – and internalized by the pupil – is likely to encourage feelings of inadequacy in the learner:

it undervalues his experience and opinions
it undervalues his own language
it undervalues talk
it overvalues writing of a particular kind – factual and impersonal
it stresses a single audience for most of the writing, the teacher perceived as an 'examiner'.

If the pupil's view of himself as a learner depends upon his teacher's view of what learning is and how he measures up to this, then clearly a change in the teacher should effect a change (in due course) in the pupil. If, instead of seeing himself as a figure of authority whose role is to test, assess and correct whatever efforts the pupil makes, the teacher sees himself as a kind of senior partner and facilitator in a mutual learning enterprise then his pupils are enabled to see themselves as valued partners, collaborators, instigators, etc. The implications of this sort of mutual teaching-learning relationship are, of course, that there will be respect for the experience, expertise, language resources etc. that each partner has to work from.

By way of illustration of some of the enabling qualities of this kind of approach, I want to refer to a story (see Martin *et al.* 1977) written by Colin, a twelve year old boy in a comprehensive school. His story was called *The Magic Marble* and his teacher gave the context for it like this:

The Magic Marble is a breakthrough story by a twelve year old boy who had been very withdrawn and rather friendless. He wrote very little and with many mistakes. We were writing 'novels' in his class and he wrote six lines – somehow I responded correctly and he did Chapter 2 – ten lines – and then proceeded to Chapter 3 and Chapter 4 till the book was finished at Chapter 21. Each chapter was written on a new page. He was very shy about it and the whole thing took about five weeks. Since a story needs an audience, I read it to the whole class who were most impressed. Then his father rang the school to say that Colin seemed very happy recently and thanked us. Since this he has been writing well, and after discussion about getting speech down on paper his writing is now almost correct, and this applies to his spelling too. Now that his story has been printed as a pamphlet it's been used very successfully with pupils in remedial withdrawal classes. I gave it to a young West Indian boy for half-term and he came back after the holiday raving to 'write' his own. This is now on tape waiting to be transcribed.

Colin's story began:

The Magic Marble

Chapter 1
My name was Joe and I went to St Georges School in Ealing. One Friday I was walking along slowly when I saw a marble, I picked it up and rubbed it. Then I put it in my pocket and started to walk along South Street where I saw my cousin Jenny. I called to her. She looked around. I called again, she stopped to wait for me.

It seems that writing this story changed Colin's view of himself. What he did was valued by the teacher – not just by what she said but by what she *did* – reading it to the class, duplicating it and circulating it as a real book – an approach which evidently inspired other children too.

For pupils to acquire a positive feeling for their abilities as learners and writers – feelings on which they can build – they need to feel that the enterprises in which they are engaged are worthwhile and that their contributions are valued. This means that, as far as possible, they are writing about things which are of interest to them for a reader who is interested in what they have to say and who responds to it. Given the priority of a response to *what* is said, then it is appropriate for the teacher to take up issues about how it is said. Notice that Colin's teacher, commenting on the influence of *The Magic Marble* said: 'Since this he has been writing well, and after discussion about getting speech down on paper his writing is now almost correct, and this applies to his spelling too.'

What all this adds up to then is that significant changes in the way that pupils see themselves as learners occur where the teacher's perception of his own role enables such changes to take place. There is no doubt that pupils quickly become aware, implicitly, of the model of learning which the teacher and the school promotes and the pupils become aware of the teacher's view of them as individual learners (see Nash 1974). There is, thus, a self-fulfilling prophecy operating at two levels. What is needed is a more open situation where pupils can find their own strategies for learning under the guidance of a teacher who values their efforts and cooperates with them.

The fictional Sissy Jupe and the real Nobby both suffered from a view of themselves as inadequate learners precisely because they were unable to conform to the model of learning which their teachers promoted (and which they accepted). And nothing else was open to them. We don't know how many such pupils there are in our schools. Nor do we know how many are more adept at concealing their lack of understanding behind successful aping of textbook and teacher.

REFERENCES

BRITTON, J. N. *et al.* (1975) *The Development of Writing Abilities 11–18* Basingstoke, England: Macmillan Education

DES (1975) *A Language for Life* (Bullock Report) London: Her Majesty's Stationery Office

MARTIN, N., D'ARCY, P., NEWTON, B., PARKER, R. (1976) *Writing and Learning Across the Curriculum 11–16* London: Ward Lock Educational

MEAD, G. H. (1934) *Mind, Self and Society* Chicago: University of Chicago Press

NASH, P. (1974) *Classrooms Observed* London: Routledge and Kegan Paul

NOTES

1 For a fuller account of an interview with Nobby see Martin, N., D'Arcy, P., Newton, B. *Language Policies for Schools: A Crucial Issue from the Bullock Report* London: Ward Lock Educational (forthcoming).

2 Goffman, E. (1974) *Asylums* Harmondsworth, England: Penguin. Goffman includes boarding schools in his examples of total institutions because all aspects of life (sleep, play and work) are conducted in the same place and under the same single authority. Day schools are not total institutions because this breakdown of barriers separating these three spheres of life does not occur. However, the practice of setting homework, the insistence on a uniform (common in English schools) and the efforts made to impose school disciplines on out-of-school behaviour are ways in which the school can be seen to attempt to extend its influence.

3 In an article 'An approach to the study of curricula as socially-organized knowledge' (in Young, M. F. D. (1974) (Ed.) *Knowledge and Control*, Collier-Macmillan) Young characterizes 'high-status knowledge' as having the following organizing principles: '... literacy, or an emphasis on written as opposed to oral presentation; individualism (or avoidance of group work or cooperativeness) ... abstractness of the knowledge and its structuring and compartmentalizing independently of the knowledge of the learner; finally and linked to the former is what I have called the unrelatedness of academic curricula, which refers to the extent to which they are "at odds" with daily life and common experience.'

4 For a fuller account see Newton, B., 'A language for life – or school?' in *Language and Learning in the Humanities* London: Ward Lock Educational.

5 The effect of just this kind of model of school learning is evident in another pupil's remark that: 'I love reading books, any kind of book as long as it's in story form and not discussional or scientific or educational.' (Jill)

81

'A slowly developing friendship': learning about writing by doing it

Robert P. Parker, Jnr

> If a teacher is to succeed in this (helping students learn to write) he will need to learn all he can about the processes involved in writing and above all the satisfactions to be derived from it.[1]

The truth of this statement, which appears in the Bullock Report chapter on 'Written language', seems obvious. Of course we need to know all we can about 'the processes involved in writing' and 'the satisfactions to be derived from it' if we are to help students develop their writing abilities. Yet, like many statements about teaching which appear so obviously true, we seldom stop to consider the truth fully, nor do we draw out sharply and seriously the implications such statements may have for our teaching. Instead, we continue to teach as we have taught, or have been taught, and occasionally we complain about the gap between theory and practice as if the gap were someone else's fault and not our own. To a considerable extent the gap *is* our fault and not someone else's. Few of us examine such abstract 'truths' carefully, nor do we systematically draw out their implications for our practice.

What, then, does this statement from the Bullock Report mean? First, the phrase 'processes involved in writing' probably pushes each of us in a different direction from that set by our training and our teaching practices. We were taught to grade products – finished pieces of writing – and much time and energy goes into doing this, or discussing how to do it. We have been trained also to teach students the 'rules' for successful composing: correct grammar, mechanics and usage; certain rhetorical principles of invention and organization; and specific methods of developing paragraphs and essay (i.e. description, narration, argumentation, comparison/contrast, persuasion etc.). 'How to' and 'whether it's good or bad' are our central concerns.

The composing *process* implies something quite different: a concern with what 'naturally' happens, what a writer 'naturally' does, from the moment he first has a thought about writing something, through whatever planning, writing and rewriting he undertakes, to the point in time when he decides that the piece he has written is finished. Thus, understanding the composing process implies observing what writers, including student writers, actually do when they compose and finding some way to describe what is observed. The approach is descriptive, not prescriptive. It suggests that we build up a picture of the composing process from looking at reality, not by borrowing a model from a textbook.

Fortunately, we now have some revealing investigations of the composing processes of student writers to add to the descriptions of their own writing professional writers have given us.[1] These studies tell us some interesting things about how students actually write. For example, each individual composes rather differently from each other individual. Each person has his own special writing conditions, including writing instruments, which are helpful or necessary for successful composing. Each person plans, composes, and revises in relatively unique ways. Moreover, the composing process differs greatly for out-of-school writing as against in-school writing. In schools, because of the uniform conditions and procedures for composing demanded by teachers and textbooks, students plan less, compose faster, and revise less. Also, their writing tends to be less personal and less experimental, more written to a formula which they hope will meet their teachers' expectations.

Helpful as these studies of the composing process are in providing insight for teachers who genuinely wish to learn all they can about the 'processes involved in writing', they still present secondhand experience, someone else's formulation. In my experience, teachers learn more about the nature and variability of the composing process faster, and with greater impact on their own approach to writing in the classroom, when they themselves write regularly. If, in addition to writing regularly in a variety of modes, they share their writing with other teachers who are also writing, and if they keep notes on their own composing process and discuss these processes in detail, they can then profitably compare their experiences with those described by researchers.

This sequence provides teachers with a context, a personal framework, for making sense of the research and applying it to their teaching.

Journal-keeping has proved valuable in this regard. At first many individuals feel awkward, directionless, even daunted by the blank page. They want to know what a journal is, what to write in it, what it is supposed to be for – all the same questions students ask. Soon, though, most people begin to take hold and to use this mode of writing for their own purposes. They write down thoughts, feelings, events, quotes from books, bits of conversation: things they wish to record permanently. They vent strong feelings and criticism which they need to express. They explore ideas encountered in books or class discussions or other conversations in an attempt to make sense of them. They formulate plans for teaching or research or other writing. They write the first drafts of poems, stories, scenes for plays. And they reflect on their own growth as people and teachers.

Because many have never written *for themselves* before, this is the first time that writing has served *their* purposes. They had always written for their teachers, and so, aside from getting a good grade, writing had always served their teachers' purposes – which were mostly to test their knowledge of required material.

Eventually, most people discover a variety of exciting and important uses for their journals. I am most interested, though, in the times when teachers use their journals to reflect on the experience of writing itself, especially on the new role that writing has begun to take on in their lives. These following few journal excerpts show teachers doing just this: reflecting on what writing can mean or can do.

(The journal excerpts which follow are presented exactly as they were originally written. Nothing has been changed, including the spacing.)

Teacher A
I feel that after the hectic of a long day, I should have time to write. It's funny, the importance that writing has taken on for

me. It's like a slowly developing friendship. After a while there's a dependency & a need to see (write) each other frequently.

I like Peter Elbow's *Writing Without Teachers*: it puts me at ease in writing down my own thoughts, as well as makes me feel more confident about 'teaching' writing to high school students. I sometimes find myself walking down sidewalks pondering, how can I *get* children to write, when I *honestly* don't write myself. Reading Elbow I want to write again. After 2 pages of his book, I closed the cover & wrote 2 free writing exercises. I enjoyed them both although the topics weren't 'enjoyable'. I kind of rediscovered what writing had meant to me before, a vent for my problems, a way of laughing at myself, relaxing, unwinding & finally learning.

Teacher A has written for herself before; and, as she starts to write again, she rediscovers the uses she had found for writing in the past. 'Getting' students to write, as she comes to see it now, may really be more a matter of helping *them* to discover these same natural human uses for writing than it is a matter of setting topics, giving instructions on form or technique, and making the evaluative criteria clear. These latter activities assume the need for extrinsic motivation; they assume that the intent to write has to be supplied by a stimulus which comes from outside the writer. Her own experience tells her the opposite: intrinsic motivation is necessary for meaningful writing. Though she may not realize it, she is questioning a stimulus-response view of the composing process.

Teacher B

My u.c. [University College, Rutgers] tutee brought me some papers from Freshman English to show me the kinds of mistakes he makes. There were two, one from each of two teachers. There was not one positive comment on either of them. No wonder he lacks confidence. We talked and I assigned topics for him to write on which had real meaning for him. There were far fewer mistakes in these papers. 'What makes you angry?' 'Tell me about your wife, kids'. On the wife paper, he made only two minor errors. By the time he wrote that for me,

I was not marking mistakes except for a circle . . . no xs, no negative comments. Then he told me why he thought I'd put the circles there. He was teaching himself. This is the first practical application of what I'm learning, and I'm delighted.

New recognition on my part, as I sit down, collect materials on which I've made notes for this entry.

I've always been secure in the belief that psychotherapy with it's nondirective techniques can help certain kinds of people with certain kinds of problems . . . qualifying the statement because I don't think I can talk about really sick people, but people trouble, neurotic, unhappy. . . . Believe that group work in a therapeutic setting is a most valuable tool . . . there is need, which I've recognized for some time, for me to take a course in group dynamics. . . . Which B.G. and I discussed the other day at MCC, and he didn't understand how I could want to use groupwork concepts, after I told him about my own spongelike attitude as a student. (This was a kind of question which lead to my rethinking the whole area and coming up with this new recognition.) I have been operating on a dichotomous view of people . . . we can learn inner truths about our psyches through nondirective, supportive techniques, but we must learn cognitively through more routinized, less individual methods. This is probably WRONG. And I've always seen myself as anti-mind/ body split . . . but have been operating on the premise that there is a real emotional/cognitive split. Thank you, B.P., and B.G.

Writing this journal is a marvelous, and unique, experience. As with some of the poetry I've written, I find myself in new situations . . . find I've learned something about myself, simply by writing about things which are even possibly tangential to it.

Teacher B realizes something different; *form*-less writing – that is, writing without a particular *form*-al product as its goal – permits self-learning to occur. She writes to record, explore, clarify her experience, and almost without knowing it, she writes herself into 'new situations'. If she were forced to make an outline in advance, to specify beforehand the direction or structure or content of her writing, these 'new situations' could not occur. Their possibility would have been planned away by the typical prewriting activities of carefully defining and limiting a topic, stating main ideas, selecting relevant details, and making a tight sentence outline. When she sits down to write, she does 'collect materials on which (she has) made notes for this entry', but this is a personal, flexible preparation – her process – and not a textbook prescription.

Teacher C
I'm getting to rather enjoy this sitting down at the typewriter without any idea of what I'm going to write. It's giving me some sort of practical basis for stating my theory. . . .

Now, let's see, I've decided I want to make a statement about English Education, and then see if I can substantiate it or compare it to what is going on now to illustrate that what I *feel* is better can be shown to be better. I OK, I believe that learning takes place at a much greater rate when we are talking or writing than when we are listening. And I feel writing about what we've read and talking about what we've seen and heard and read are essential steps in truly understanding what we've read or heard and making it meaningful to ourselves. . . .

When we try to voice our beliefs, we find them stronger or see gaps in reasoning that must be filled in, we learn *as* we talk and listen to others talk and respond to what we've said. In the traditional method, supposedly the learning takes place prior to the speech and the speech is the 'presenting' of what has been learned. In this latter method, the learning goes on during speech, it evolves out of our talk. It is not 'presenting' but 'sharing'. . . .

In much the same way, the English curriculum uses writing as merely 'packaging' for what has supposedly been learned beforehand. It is the means by which we present what we have learned to the teacher. . . . We learn in the process of creating. We learn by talking and writing. Over and over again I've read these statements, and more and more I experience the truth of what I'm reading. . . . See, once again I wrote and clarified things for myself. I used to dread this writing. I might even begin to really, really enjoy it someday!

As Robert Frost said, 'No surprise for the writer, no surprise for the reader'. No wonder so much school writing sounds dull, empty, lifeless. It is, with good reason, totally without surprise for the reader. The very structure of composing that most grammar/composition textbooks present makes surprise, discovery, writing as an heuristic process, impossible. As Janet Emig (1971) says of *Warriner's*, typical of such books, it 'suggests writing is a tidy, accretive affair that proceeds by elaborating a fully preconceived and formulated plan'. Writing which follows this model becomes, as Teacher c realizes, merely a process of 'packaging' a preformulated message. If the writer must know exactly what she is going to say before she writes, she will not anticipate the possibility of being able to learn *from* her writing, or to say, as Teacher c did, 'See, once again I wrote and clarified things for myself'.

Because these teachers *are* writers now, they know that writing brings surprise, discovery, when it serves their purposes. These purposes may be fleeting as 'relaxing, unwinding' or as permanent as confronting one's ideas about nondirective vs. directive teaching. Regardless, their needs or wishes must give rise to the writing if it is to have meaning for them. Even then, the writing may bring no satisfaction – no shape or meaning or insight or outlet. There is no guarantee either way, though writing for someone else's purposes is less likely to be satisfying.

As these teachers also realize, some writing involves 'presenting' rather than 'sharing' ideas. Sometimes we need to write more impersonally in order to convey ideas that have already been developed, data that have been organized and interpreted, arguments that have been carefully formulated. If students experience writing nearly always as being impersonal and presentative, though, it seems unlikely that they will ever learn, as a fourth teacher (D) wrote, 'a lot about the *value* of writing'. They may never see that 'without it (writing), ideas are diffused and scattered and it becomes much harder to pinpoint and clarify things . . . there's only a limited number or range of ideas that (we) can hold on to at one time and if (we) don't write them down as they come, they're gone'.

Teacher D

Perhaps the problem with teachers allowing and helping students to find ways of learning through writing is that the teachers themselves don't know how to do it. Until now, I had never found in writing anything more than a means to a finished product which would in some way be evaluated. Even now, it's hard for me to think of using writing for *me*. I'm conscious even as I'm writing this that at some time someone will read it. It seems obvious, then, that without a lot more practice, I'm going to have a hard time helping others towards learning through writing. It's not that I can't see the value – because I *can* – but that I don't know how to do it. Without the courses I've had here, I wouldn't even have been aware that such a possibility existed. I still think of writing as 'something which happens *after* the learning'.

I sense in the journal excerpts a further insight about how writing ability develops. Teacher B comes nearest to it when she describes working with her adult college tutee. As she observed, he made far fewer errors when he wrote on topics 'which had real meaning for him'.

The Bullock Report makes this same point in a more general way:

The solution lies in a recognition on the part of teachers that a writer's intention is prior to his need for techniques. The teacher who aims to extend the pupil's power as a writer must therefore work first upon his intentions, and *then* upon the techniques appropriate to them. (p. 164)

Matters of technique become important to Teacher B's tutee, when he has an 'intention' of his own that he wants to realize, or work out, in writing. Most errors disappear and he cares about understanding and eliminating those that remain. When he writes on required topics that do not draw on his intentions, he cares less about technique, makes more errors. His regular teachers probably think he doesn't *know how* to write correctly, when the truth is, he does.

It has always seemed to me to be the case that we learn, or employ, skills most fully in the process of doing *something else* – working towards some end other than skill learning – that we care about. Unfortunately, though, as Margaret Spencer (1975) points out about the discussion of reading in the Bullock Report:

> The dominant view is that skills have to be taught. The alternative, that children can, and do, take the process in hand for themselves if the operation is meaningful enough, appears only here and there.

If she is right, if children do 'take the process (of reading) in hand for themselves' when it serves their purposes, might this not also be true for learning to write? It does seem as if Teacher B's tutee takes the writing process in hand when he writes to fulfil his intentions.

How, then, can teachers reach this understanding? Certainly, they can learn by reading articles such as the one by Margaret Spencer and books like the Bullock Report. Such learning, as I have pointed out above, is abstract and secondhand. How can teachers bridge the 'gap' between this generalized, secondhand knowledge and their own intentions and actions? In the passage below, Nancy Martin (1976) suggests one way that this happens, first by quoting from James Britton and then in her own words.

> . . . the practitioner does not merely apply; he must re-formulate from the general starting points supplied by the research and arrive at new ends – new not only to him but new in the sense that they are not part of the research findings, being a discovery of a different order.
>
> Thus we see the relationship between research and teaching as the rehypothesizing of research findings by teachers in the light of the meanings built up from their past experiences.

It is these 'past experiences' that worry me. How many teachers have had experiences with writing similar to the ones these teachers describe in their journals. How many teachers value writing *as a means of learning*? More than that, though, how many have experienced writing *as a whole process*: first as a means of locating and clarifying their intentions, and then as a means of finding the techniques to realize their intentions in a form which makes sense to them and communicates with others?

The best example of this entire process that I have at hand begins in Teacher D's journal, kept for a course entitled 'Developing a theory of education in English', and ends with the original theoretical paper which she, along with other students, was required to write.

Teacher D Journal entries
September 9, 1976
What I believe is fundamental about teaching English or anything else is, I think, reflected in the two things I wrote in class:

> Man learns by making connections between what is inside him and what is outside him.
>
> Teaching is finding ways to help people make those connections. I believe that the emphasis on 'inside' or 'outside' varies according to the particular 'subject' or 'task' or 'content' or whatever – the what-is-to-be-learned. If I am learning/ teaching astronomy, there is more outside than inside. My head simply does not contain astronomy until someone teaches it to me. *But*, if there is not point of connection (relevance, the 'ahha' experience, whatever one may call it), I will not *learn* about astronomy. I may be able to recite facts for a short time, but the facts will not be *mine* and I will not have *learned*.

I do not believe that learning involves only thinking nor only feeling. Just as connections must be made between what is inside and what is outside, so also must connections be made among all of what is inside. If what I think is not what I feel (if the two are not congruent), I cannot learn or teach as a whole person until I have made some connections.

In this first excerpt, written after the initial meeting of the course in September, we can see her already thinking about the idea of learning as a process of 'making connections between what is inside . . . and what is outside'. It seems obvious that she has 'had' this idea before, though this may be her first attempt to formulate it carefully. She also provides an example, using herself as the subject, and adds an important qualification: 'Just as connections must be made between what is inside and what is outside, so also must connections be made among all of what is inside.'

September 13, 1976
p. 26, *W and L** 'the vital learning process – that of making links between what is already known and the new information'
'known' needs to include what is sensed and felt as well as what is already digested by the intellect – this is what I mean by *making connections. . . .*

I'm left now, though with a feeling that I need some new direction in which to move in order to make this 'theory' become mine and become specifically related to some aspect of English.

In the second entry, written a week later, she has found support for her idea in a book we were all reading for the course. And here again she adds another important qualification: the connections we make—what we 'know' – can be 'sensed' or 'felt' as well as understood consciously, explicitly, intellectually.

September 27, 1976
I think this class taught me some things about my own learning that I didn't know before . . . I had a theory. I sensed that if I took it in the direction of writing, the book we're reading had done it better. If I went towards reading, Louise Rosenblatt had done it better. I didn't know where else it might go. What I wanted was specific direction; what I got at first was sympathy ('Now, now, just because other people have done it doesn't mean you can't.' Pat, pat on the head.) I sensed my

---

* This refers to Nancy Martin *et al.* (1976) *Writing and Learning Across the Curriculum 11–16* London: Ward Lock Educational

resentment but didn't know how to do the redirect. The specific suggestion of working with talk was a move in the helpful direction, I thought, but not quite what I really wanted to do. After all, I spend too much of my day *avoiding* little kids' talk to want to go looking for it. So I left class feeling just as frustrated as when I came.

But on the way home I realized something about making connections as I started making some myself. My real interest is in student questions (not my *only* real interest). If we learn by making connections between what is outside and what is inside, we must learn (or know) how to ask effective questions. Questions can be one way to make such connection. Is there some way I can use the ideas about questions in working toward a theory?

By the third week, she is beginning to feel frustrated by the process of theory construction, and resentful of what she sees as a condescending response to her predicament. None the less, she is still thinking about the idea of learning as making inside/outside connections, and has added another dimension to her sense of what she wants to do with this idea. She has made an 'inner connection' between her fascination with the view of learning and her interest in questions, and so she has further clarified her intentions for the eventual paper. Perhaps this clarification happens because her view of learning is no longer only an abstraction. It stems from, and illuminates, her *personal experience*, as well as what she takes to be the experience of others; it is both a personal insight *and* a theoretical idea, and thus she is committeed to it in a way that provides intent and energy for her paper.

October 11, 1976
I *do* want to begin with some actual observations of questions as they are actually asked, not with a theory that I pull out of the air or out of my head.

I believe that people learn by making connections between what is inside and what is outside. I believe that some kinds of questions help people make these connections because they arise from some gap between what is already inside and something sensed or observed or whatever outside. I may call these 'learning questions'.

There are probably several kinds of utterances which could be learning questions but not all of those grammatical utterances which are questions will result in learning. . . .

The slant I want to represent is from the area of making connections, but I do not know how to word what I want to say.

I think that the 'connections' idea and the emphasis on the importance of questions are closely related to Kelly's* theory.

Do I have to classify *all* questions before I can identify one particular kind to work with?

The fundamental postulate is not a statement about the questions. It is the idea that learning is making connections between what is inside and what is outside. What is what is basic. I am then theorizing that there are certain kinds of questions – I am calling them 'learning questions' – that facilitate making these connections for an individual learner. What are the characteristics of these questions? Are they grammatical constructions? Or would a *statement* sometimes qualify as a 'learning question'?

Back to this fundamental postulate business.

People learn by connections what is inside with
what is outside.
outer events

'Learning' questions facilitate this process. The observable characteristics of L.Q.'s are. . . .

recognition

L.Q.'s indicate a person's awareness of a gap between inside & outside at a particular moment and a desire to acknowledge or bridge that gap.

– a desire for connection –

hypothesis: the asking of a larger # of L.Q.'s indicates a greater awareness of one's own learning process and less reliance on outside stimuli to produce 'learning' . . . is desirable.

hypothesis: there are ways of increasing the #s of learning questions which a person asks.

* Kelly, G. (1963) *A Theory of Personality* New York: Norton

hyp: stimulation of L.Q.'s would lead to more learning and more awareness of one's own learning process.

Here, four weeks later, she was still making connections, still making intentions for this paper more exact. We would typically call this process defining a topic; but, it seems to me, it is not a topic *per se* that she was after. She had that in her first journal entry. Rather, she was searching for what it was that she wanted to say about the topic – and not at all in the sense of outlining main ideas or selecting relevant details.

The journal provided a perfect vehicle for this search. It offered a place for personal, open-ended, tentative writing. In it she could speculate, hypothesize, argue, exclaim, digress, even fantasize, and nothing she said would be held against her. Because of what she had done in her journal, she knew what she wanted to do in the paper when she began to write. Her intention had become clear, and she could attend to such techniques as organization, analysis, argument, use of detail etc which would make her paper 'good'. Here is a brief excerpt which gives a sense of the overall paper.

Teacher D

If a man is a learning being, as Kelly and others have suggested that he is, then why do we need schools at all? Why not just let people go through life learning as they will? I believe that there is a purpose for school though the purposes which may be a natural outgrowth of the view of learning presented here may be quite different from the purposes which schools now serve. I would 'propose that schooling be liberating in contrast to controlling; that the basic goal be the development of autonomous, valuing human beings, not . . . role-oriented skills'. School could and should be a special form of enriching experiences different from what could be had if one were to wander through life making random connections as they happened to occur. These experiences should also be different from totally inward-looking psychotherapy, which may produce learning not of a kind appropriate to the schools I envision. Richard Jones's distinction between insight and outsight may be useful here. In pyschotherapy, one seeks insight, for its own sake. In school, insight is valuable as a way to achieve outsight; in other words, the purpose of school is not to promote connections between a person and his own inner structures (though these connections are learning and are valuable) but to promote connections between a person's inner structure and his outer experiences. It is in the richness and diversity of these outer experiences which it may provide that school has its special function.

Perhaps the model of learning proposed by Macdonald, Wolfson and Zaret will be helpful as we explore what schools might be. They suggest that learning occurs in three stages: exploring, integrating, and transcending. In the exploring phase, there is a free and intuitive interaction with the environment. The exploring is internally experienced and is active. John Holt calls it 'messing around' and argues that it gives children experience, a context, a framework into which they can fit new concepts or problems. The integrating phase involves preliminary structuring and is tentative. It is this phase of learning that is most often exploited in schools, as students are pushed prematurely to generalize and to talk of concepts (even if they have not yet internalized the concepts). Forming hypotheses is one way of making guesses about connection; if schools reward certainty and penalize tentativeness, they ignore the likelihood that all learning or insight is tentative at first. As Holt describes it: 'All of us must cross the line between ignorance and insight many times before we truly understand. Not only must we cross that line many times, but . . . nobody else can cross it for us. . . . Being shoved or dragged across does no good.' Of central importance is the active trying out of concepts and models which are developed as a result of exploring. Often the process of making connections is not an immediate, easy flash of insight, but is a struggle, a slow working through and around. If this process is not given time to happen, there can be no learning. Rushing abstractions before the student himself is ready for them will not work:

You must wait until they are willing reflectively to turn around before you begin operating with the abstractions.

Otherwise they will become obedient and noncomprehending . . . I put this matter first for I feel that it is the one thing that children most rarely encounter in school—that it is a good practice to *use* their head to solve a problem by reflecting on what they already know or have already learned.

The transcending phase is insightful knowing. It is making connections. It is the culmination of learning. Because it has originated within the student it is relevant. It takes the student where he has not been before because it is his own grasping, his own comprehending. It will not be forgotten because it has a place in the student's inner structures.

Writing not only involves processes, it is a process – of thinking as well as writing. Writing tentatively, at length, over time, without evaluation, before formulating a finished piece for public reading allows the process to occur in its fullest, most instrumental form. Teacher D wrote her journal to learn about something – in this case, learning as making connection – and in the process learned something about writing as well. This, I think, is the way it happens best: we learn to write most quickly and most fully when we write to learn about something.

. . . as long as our gaze is almost exclusively on language . . . the teachers' intentions and the children's intentions will seldom coincide. 'For the intentions which pupils have that lead them into language acts are not intentions about language but about "content" – that is, about *something*: thing, idea, memory, feeling, fantasy image, book, that they want to tell someone about or find out from someone about. So to arrive at some useful ideas on how to get the intentions happening it would be necessary to give some thought to the world of "what is talked about".' Language in action cannot be separated from what it is used for and with what intent, and whose intent.[2] (Martin 1976)

How might you come to know this? By writing to learn yourself. By going through the process, not just for the sake of going through it, not just as an exercise, but because there is something to understand, to work out, which writing can help you with.

These I think, are the implications of the two passages from Bullock that I have quoted above. And now it is up to you. What do you think? What does your experience of writing tell you? Try writing about these and other issues and see what 'new situations' you find yourselves in.

REFERENCES

MARTIN, N. (1976) Language across the curriculum: a paradox and its potential for change *Educational Review* 11

SPENCER, M. (1975) (with Moira McKenzie) 'Learning to read and the reading process' in H. Rosen (Ed.) *Language and Literacy in Our Schools: Some Appraisals of the Bullock Report* London: University of London Institute of Education

NOTES

1 See in particular Janet Emig's (1971) pioneering study *The Composing Processes of Twelfth Graders* Urbana, Illinois: National Council of Teachers of English, also Donald Graves (1975) The composing processes of seven-year-olds *Research in the Teaching of English*, September

4 Implications from the Report for teacher training

INTRODUCTION

Each contributor to this section examines the professional development of teachers *as people*. Teachers, they say, are people with specific skills which enable them to help others develop. Neither learning nor applying these helping skills occurs by adherence to a set of rules, whether simple or complex. Rather, this learning comes about through a process involving deep commitment to one's own growth, relationships with skilled helpers, and finally, an integration of personal, social, literate and communicative abilities with the professional role.

Chris Crowest emphasizes the necessity for prospective teachers to approach teaching through practical work. For critics who see education courses as nonchallenging, he maintains that these can be as rigorous as any theoretical study. The very act of applying what one learns as theory requires both a knowledge of that theory and a thinking through of how best to apply it in relation to particular groups of students.

Learning how to integrate theory and personal knowledge is a developmental process. Both Kathryn Miller and Chris Crowest discuss how teacher-training programmes might be planned to accommodate student growth as it develops. Miller suggests a series of six underlying components for such a programme which assists this development and fits the Bullock recommendations. These include, among other things, a broad base of child-development understanding. Crowest is more specific about the course work in such a programme, and illustrates by describing a course plan he designed and implemented at Dartford College of Education. He emphasizes a fundamental learning principle: that it is through 'the practice of a variety of skills and the development of many interests that language becomes an integral part of the learning process'.

Miller suggests the personal literacy development of teachers should receive greater attention from colleges of education.

There may be two reasons for this lack in emphasis, at least in America: large lecture classes which discourage verbal interaction, and a preoccupation with multiple-choice tests and short-answer quizzes. These practices tend to break down efforts to foster the development of literate abilities in would-be teachers. Because the focus is on a 'quick' exhibition of knowledge rather than on asking students to think about relationships, it becomes difficult for students to develop the feeling that society places a high value on the kinds of verbal thinking which are at the heart of literacy. Those who are unable to see the value of literacy for themselves are not likely to be interested in developing the literate abilities of others.

Because he is active in speech and communication training and involved in educational programmes which help teachers learn communicative principles, Don Ecroyd writes from a different perspective than the other two authors in this section. He sees literacy as a part of communication – not communication as a part of literacy. Communication, as a process of open symbolic interaction, involves learning how to make wise choices about the best way to present material to listeners. Ecroyd also encourages teachers to approach their teaching from an investigative stance. His concept of the scientist-teacher is similar to the idea Bob Parker proposes in section 6 for action-research. Ecroyd, however, suggests the systematic use of behaviour theory for the scientist-teacher. In his view, the skills of planning behavioural objectives should be learned in teacher-education programmes. These skills can then enable teacher-scientists to experiment with a wide range of instructional strategies.

Bullock and teacher-education programmes in America

Kathryn Madera Miller

Everyone who has some idea about what is wrong – or right – with the educational process or with the products of education has many ideas about 'fixing' or 'improving' the process or product through 'better' education of teachers. The authors of the Bullock Report join this group of 'suggesters' by offering fourteen recommendations for the preservice training of teachers and seventeen recommendations for inservice training.

It seems we are expecting more and more of our teachers just as we are expecting more and more of children. In turn we expect more and more of teachers-in-training. We develop long lists of competencies and then plan equally long lists of courses or special experiences aimed at developing the competencies. Teacher-training programmes have become longer through the years as we plan more and more to be included in the preservice programme. Katz (1972) writes of the developmental stages of teachers and suggests our teacher-training programmes often do not reflect these developmental stages. Most organized academic programmes concern themselves essentially with the preservice training although state certification requirements mandate continuing education.

Perhaps since teacher-training institutions have more 'control' over the preservice years, we insist *everything* must be found in that preservice training. Looking at the lengthy list of recommendations in the Bullock Report and participating in some lively curriculum discussions here in America, I am often led to the discouraging conclusion that if students are really to *prepare* for teaching they will be too old to teach by the time that preparation is completed! Are any of us *really* prepared for the tasks we face? Can we look at ourselves and others more kindly and positively by recognizing preparing to teach and teaching, as well as teaching and learning, as intertwined in the experience of living? If development begins at conception and ends at death, perhaps it can be said that teacher training begins at conception and ends at death!

The Bullock Report recognizes the many faces of life and learning by listing conclusions and recommendations going well beyond those identified as for teacher training. To me several of their conclusions and recommendations not specifically directed at teacher training also have implications for American teacher education. Now I join the list of those who suggest an outline of teacher education. This list is limited to six interrelated components with the belief that these are supported by the Bullock Report and the firm conviction that different individuals at each of the developmental stages of teachers (Katz) may be working with these components in different ways.

COMPETENCE IN WORKING WITH PARENTS

The authors of the Plowden Report (DES (1967)) emphasized the importance of parents when they identified parental attitudes as contributing more to the variation in educational performance than home circumstances or the state of the school (Table 1, p. 33). The Bullock Report echoes this conclusion and presents several recommendations aimed at parents and at school personnel and others working with parents.

But we all know that, you say? We know that parents are important, but what has that to do with teacher education? We are to discuss here teacher education and not parent education? To me working with parents is one cornerstone of good teaching and one that too frequently, at least until recently, has been ignored or left for teachers to 'learn on the job'. Several years ago at a conference, when I suggested it is important to help the college student learn to work with parents and other adults, someone replied that such a scheme is fruitless because teachers, especially those who choose to work with young children, are largely ineffectual with adults and for that reason have withdrawn into the world of children. I refuse to accept that idea!

I firmly agree with the Bullock Report Summary of Conclusions and Recommendations #40: 'Parents should be helped to understand the process of language development in their children and to play their part in it' and #70: 'Parents have an extremely important part to play in preparing the child for the early stages of reading.' No, the Report does not make teachers solely responsible for helping parents to reach this understanding, but it does recognize the part teachers and schools have to play in such a process. Teachers today, especially of young children, must be ready and willing, or better yet eager, to work with parents and a variety of other agencies also working with parents. I find it difficult today to talk only about working with children; working with children and their families seems more accurate and appropriate.

And in what ways does the Bullock Committee suggest teachers work with parents? Their list includes home visiting, parent participation in the classroom and the gradual entry of children into groups. In my experience, preservice teachers do not recall such practices from their own early days and tend to be hesitant about trying them or sceptical of their worth. Perhaps they have just never thought at all about doing these things.

Therefore, I recommend that all preservice education programmes include not only knowledge of a wide variety of ways of contacting and working with parents, but also opportunity to practise these methods. In addition, there should be extensive contact with working teachers who use such methods enthusiastically although they are cognisant of the limitations of a home-school programme.

ABILITY TO WORK WITH A VARIETY OF AGENCIES AND AGE GROUPS
The Bullock Report charges other agencies besides presecondary schools with the responsibility for working with parents. Students in secondary schools are suggested as appropriate audiences for preparental education. It is strongly recommended that such programmes for the secondary student include actual work with children in nursery schools, day-care centres and other such places of contact with the young child. The teacher of young children must then also be prepared with the knowledge and attitudes to work effectively with the students of the secondary school.

Bullock also charges health agencies, TV, libraries, adult-education programmes etc. with aiding parents in becoming more aware of their role in the education of their children and helping them develop skills and confidence as effective teaching parents. Teacher-education programmes might well examine community agencies working with parents to expand their awareness of the teacher-in-training but also to suggest appropriate nonclassroom employment for those educated to work with young children.

STRONG BASIC KNOWLEDGE AND UNDERSTANDING OF HUMAN DEVELOPMENT

Ability to provide sound emotional climate and aid in development of positive self-concepts
But how can we ask a teacher of young children to work with all age groups, you ask? How can preservice education possibly prepare a young student (or even a mature one) to work with so many different people in so many different capacities? Probably none can but is it not the purpose of preservice education to provide a foundation on which later learnings can grow? Surely self-understanding and knowledge of human development are a part of this foundation.

The Bullock Report does indeed stress the need for knowledge and understanding of the child and the developmental processes. Certainly the need for a positive self-concept is recognized in Bullock's Conclusions and Recommendations section:

109 A child's accent should be accepted and attempts should not be made to suppress it. The aim should be to provide him with awareness and flexibility.

68 The majority of pupils need a great deal of positive help to develop the various comprehension skills to a high level.

86 Individual attention should not be confined to poor readers, for average and above average children also need it if they are to make optimal progress.

214 Intellectual capacity affects a child's ability to acquire linguistic skills, but as intelligence itself is a developmental concept any child can be expected to make considerable gains with good teaching, sustained support and positive expectations on the part of the school.

Learning how to create a climate for healthy emotional development should be a strong part of any programme of pre-service education for the teachers of young children.

Bullock also emphasizes that 'good teaching' must be based on the cognitive processes in the developing child. The Report lists some conclusions teachers, other school personnel and particularly some curriculum writers seem to forget:

108 Exploratory talk by the pupils has an important function in the process of learning.

36 Language has a unique role in developing human learning: the higher processes of thinking are normally achieved by the interaction of a child's language behaviour with his other mental and perceptual powers.

37 Children learn as certainly by talking and writing as by listening and reading.

38 The surest means by which a child is enabled to discover his mother tongue is by exploiting the process of discovery through language in all its uses.

Surely teacher-education programmes must not deny the above by concentrating on a variety of ways to 'keep children quiet'! We might add:

73 It should be established from the beginning in the mind of the child that reading is primarily a thinking process, not simply an exercise in identifying shapes and sounds.

Do we teach preservice teachers that teaching and learning are thinking processes? Or do we teach that learning is primarily the memorization of words and that teaching is primarily following the directions provided with commercial teaching materials? Do we work at keeping teachers-in-training quiet while they listen to us tell them they should help children express themselves? What models do college teachers provide for preservice teachers?

SKILL IN OBSERVATION

Observation of children (and adults) is one way to help teachers-in-training to learn about human development but observation itself is a vital teaching skill for all to develop. The teacher observes and plans on the basis of observations, observes the plans in operation with children, observes changes and then plans again. In the words of the Bullock Report, #205: 'Expert observation cannot be valued too highly; it is a major teaching skill and one upon which all effective diagnosis is founded. . . .' Here the Report goes on to relate the observation and diagnosis specifically to language development, but is not careful observation of use in all areas of development and all parts of a school curriculum?

Extensive observation and help in writing and interpreting observations to improve skill in observation and in wise use of information gained must be an integral part of teacher-education programmes. Are teachers-in-training observing children? Are they keeping written records of their observations? Are college instructors reading the observations and making suggestions to the students which aid them in increasing their ability to observe more fruitfully? Do the students grow in their ability to observe more precisely, write observations richer in detail, and interpret their findings more acutely? Is the value of interpretation recognized at all? Are interpretations and diagnoses made on the basis of well-founded observations? Do teachers-in-training work with practising teachers who use observational records in planning their work with children? Do adults planning for children (and other adults) use their skills in observation to *really* plan for *individuals*?

Teacher skills in language
Teachers have long been recognized as models for their students (Bullock Report #111: 'The teacher's own speech is a crucial factor in developing that of his pupils.') and the need to learn by doing is documented in the Report as well as in many other places. The importance of the teacher's skill with language as well as the importance of *teachers'* positive self-concept is recognized in the Bullock Report #115:

In learning about the nature and operation of language, students should be made more explicitly aware of their own practices. Improvements in students' language performance should take place in this context rather than in 'remedial' courses.

(Here 'students' refers to teachers-in-training.) In short, to aid children in language development, teachers must possess personal skills in language as well as in understanding children and their development of language. To develop these personal skills, students, like children, must have the opportunity to explore and practise language in all its complexity. To re-examine the recommendation of the Bullock Report mentioned earlier, do our college students 'learn as certainly by talking and writing as by listening and reading'? Has the American college become more and more dependent on the large lecture where students do indeed listen and read? Instead of writing, do our students mark boxes on examination answer sheets? Such trends hardly promote skills desired in teachers of young children taking on responsibility for the development of language.

FINAL WORDS

What characteristics do *you* desire in a teacher working with children to help them develop 'a language for life'? I would seek a confident individual, with a strong self-concept and basic understanding of human development. This individual would be skilled in working with a wide variety of agencies, age groups, and individuals, including parents. In working with others the teacher would provide a sound model of language use as well as other life skills and would use observation skills to provide a climate conducive to growth for teacher and student alike. How would this be accomplished? How can we all grow? With thought. With action. Little by little . . .

REFERENCES

DES (1967) *Children and their Primary Schools Volume 1: The Report* (Plowden Report) London: Her Majesty's Stationery Office

KATZ, L. (1972) Developmental stages of preschool teachers *Elementary School Journal*, 73,1, pp. 50–54

Bullock and teacher-education programmes in Britain

Chris Crowest

THE ENGLISH TEACHER-TRAINING SYSTEM

Students preparing to teach in England's state schools are required to study for three years at a college of education recognized by the Department of Education and Science. This course of initial training leads to a certificate which allows the student to teach and which is also recognized as the first part of an ordinary degree in education. By the 1980s it is anticipated that the certificate will be phased out and replaced by the BEd Degree so that teaching will have become a graduate profession.

The courses offered to students vary in style and content from one college to another. Each academic board submits its course for validation to the Council for National Academic Awards or is part of the group of colleges associated with the University offering a certificate agreed between them.

Despite the diversity of submissions and college groupings there is a large area of agreement between colleges about basic course content. Furthermore, the Government, through the Department of Education and Science, insists that all students entering teacher-education courses should be both numerate and literate and most programmes are designed to add substantially to the students' academic development as well as providing a comprehensive professional preparation for teaching.

Most courses are subdivided within colleges to offer a difference in emphasis according to the age range the student wishes to teach. Traditionally these divisions have fallen into three main groupings: infants (5–7 years); juniors (8–11 years); secondary (11–15 years). The secondary courses normally relate to specialist studies concerned with preparing students to teach one or two academic disciplines. Additionally they offer the theory and practice of education. There may be a short course on the teaching of reading but this is often optional.

The infant and junior courses are more frequently concerned with broadly-based curriculum studies closely linked to educational theory and practice. The student also studies one academic discipline intended for his personal enrichment.

At Dartford College of Education I was responsible for a primary course. That is one which covers the age range from five to eleven: that part of the English educational schools system known as the primary school. It is the language content of that course which I mainly want to discuss in this paper.

THE AIM OF THE LANGUAGE COMPONENT

One of the most contentious issues in Certificate of Education courses is the division of time between theoretical studies in educational psychology, philosophy and sociology on the one hand and professional curriculum studies on the other. At Dartford it was agreed that the professional curriculum should occupy approximately three-fifths of the time allocation. This made it possible to plan a language unit to run concurrently with other studies but extended over eight terms, allowing for both practical and theoretical applications in college and in the classroom. The ninth term is almost entirely taken up with revision for final examinations.

The aim of the language component is to prepare students to help children of primary age towards becoming literate. The focus is upon individual development and the acquisition of those skills that a child needs to function efficiently in school.

It is assumed as a principal aim of the primary school that children should be able to read and write. Students discuss the demands of society within the content of sociological studies but essentially the concern is with reading and the enjoyment of books closely linked to studies in the development of speech and written language.

Preparation for the further stages of education and the eventual demands of adult life are important supplementary aims that lie alongside the central task of satisfying the immediate needs of the growing child.

Although during the second year of study we put the emphasis heavily upon the skills and techniques relating to the teaching of reading, the language course is broadly based. The following headings indicate aspects of the syllabus considered at one stage or another during the eight terms.

It must be emphasized that approximately half the study time is spent in schools working with children under the supervision of tutors and teachers. College time is spent in lectures, seminars, reading and practical sessions largely devoted to the preparation of reading material and other language stimuli.

Summary of the course

1 *Towards literacy* This is a discussion which concerns definitions of literacy.

2 *The essential role of the teacher* The importance of agreed school policy and the need to identify language experience. The teacher's own use of language.

3 *Early language development* The need to intervene to help structure talk.

4 *Talking and writing* The important link between the two throughout the primary school.

5 *Early stages of reading* The need to establish a balance between interest and construction. Emphasis on reading linked to experience.

6 *The development of reading schemes* Stress on matching the material to the child. Word-attack skills. Introducing phonics.

7 *Reading comprehension* The need to practise comprehension skills from the beginning. Practising the techniques that are concerned with contextual cues and extracting meaning from the text as a whole.

   The complexity for older children comes through the examination of more elaborate textual structures that deal not only with factual questions but also invite conjecture and hypothesis.

8 *Literature* The importance of narrative as a story motivation for reading. The importance of poetry, music and song.

9 *Oral language* Its significance throughout the primary school and the need for teacher intervention to stimulate and extend structures.

10 *Written language* The link between child as writer and teacher as principal recipient. Autobiography into fiction. The use of the curriculum.

11 *Marking and correcting* Reinforcement. A positive approach to rewriting.

12 *Handwriting* The need for regular practise, legibility, the satisfaction from the element of craftsmanship.

13 *Language across the curriculum* Language as an integral part of the learning process.

14 *Drama* The recognition of its substantial contribution to language development at all stages. The study of movement, puppetry and practical exercises and performances.

15 *Organization and record-keeping* Formal and informal procedures. The importance of personal contact in continuity.

16 *Spelling*

17 *Diagnostic procedures*

18 *Book provision*

19 *Technological aids*. The advantages and dangers of programmed learning schemes.

The practical element
There is no doubt that the regular weekly contact with children throughout the three years of the course is a vital and essential ingredient. Much of the theoretical work in language, psychology and sociology is extremely difficult to assimilate if students have not had the opportunity to observe and experiment in the classroom. Indeed, I am of the opinion that the lack of such substantial practical provision in some colleges is the prime reason for the inadequacy felt by many probationary teachers. It is a matter of concern that the movement towards a graduate qualification seems to be associated with a more demanding academic course that in some institutions is being interpreted as necessarily less practical. Consequently, the amount of classroom practice is being reduced. This is a sadly misplaced notion, for clearly stringent academic work can be pursued through practical observation and experiment closely linked and supported by

theoretical studies. Indeed the bulk of the research concerned with the analysis of speech structures can only be tackled in the practical classroom or language laboratory. Furthermore, there is clearly a limit to theoretical studies in reading that are not pursued alongside the child.

LANGUAGE ACROSS THE CURRICULUM

'By his training and experience the primary-school teacher is likely to conceive of his task in terms of integrated rather than subject-orientated work.' The Bullock Report acknowledged the fact that in training students to teach primary children colleges are aware of the central role language plays across the curriculum. This, of course, is a well-established principle in most English primary schools. Indeed, a concern at the present time is that the integrated approach to the curriculum should not be abandoned under the pressure to sharpen the literacy and numeracy programmes. It is not a style of teaching that would thus be threatened but a serious disregard of the way a child learns. It is through the practice of a variety of skills and the development of many interests that language becomes an integral part of the learning process. Such a fundamental principle must be preserved both in teacher-training programmes and for schools.

THE ACADEMIC FREEDOM OF TUTORS IN COLLEGES OF EDUCATION

Although the final examinations at the end of the three-year course impose certain constraints upon tutors, the course allows considerable flexibility in the manner in which it is presented.

In some colleges the emphasis in language studies will be closely linked to sociological implications. In others there will be a strong psychological bias. Furthermore, individual tutors will stress certain aspects according to their own strengths and interests, for example, of the three colleagues who strongly reflect particular elements in their teaching, one has a deep concern for literature and poetry, another is an intense advocate of phonic-skill training, and another shows a remarkable ability in linking language skills with work in drama. Such idiosyncratic teaching leads to a diversity of styles in courses. It stems from an independent, individual approach to teaching that is deeply rooted in the British school tradition. Of course, such methods both confuse and enrich our courses but many of us are prepared to tolerate some confusion in method for the obvious benefits we derive from teaching that reflects personal strengths and enthusiasms.

THE IMPORTANCE OF CONCURRENT COURSES

Recently there has been a tendency to introduce modular or unit systems into teacher-education courses. One can see the administrative tidiness and other advantages of a programme that can be presented in packages, each examined and credited independently. However, I have serious reservations about such methods. The learning process must hang together as a whole and as the student matures over the three years of the course so should the disparate threads of study be woven together. This is more likely to be achieved if the course elements are laid alongside one another on a continuum that allows for intellectual maturation and also provides time for ideas to be tested in prolonged practical and theoretical exercises.

INSERVICE TRAINING

Because of the growing complexity of a teacher's task it is becoming increasingly necessary to reinforce initial training with a support service of ongoing courses in professional studies. These are normally provided by local authorities through teachers' centres. They consist of day-release or evening studies, block courses of varying level and duration. In addition to these demanding courses – for which, incidentally, a teacher receives no academic credit or recognition – the universities offer diplomas and advanced studies leading to postgraduate qualifications in a variety of educational disciplines. Many local authorities now provide language centres where it is possible for students to examine advanced material concerned with language development and techniques relating to the teaching of reading.

It is no longer considered sufficient to invite a child to 'bark at a book' (as Dr Joyce Morris once put it) and most teachers are very conscious of the need to know as much as possible about the diagnosis of reading difficulties and the skills that are necessary to deal adequately with children in their development towards literacy.

In addition to recapitulation in depth and the diagnosis of general and specific language problems, teachers' courses tend to relate to recording and evaluation; strategies for developing language through the analysis of complex speech patterns; school library techniques and book provision linked to a deeper and more sophisticated appraisal of children's literature. There are also courses in poetry and drama.

A predominant area of serious study for teachers in the inner city is the provision of suitable material for ethnic minorities and the whole problem of changing patterns in a multiracial society and teaching English as a second language.

COLLEGE REACTION TO THE REPORT

A Language for Life has made a substantial impact upon the colleges of education. It has given fresh impetus to the continuing debate on language teaching. The recommendations made in the Report are a challenge which must be met. It will be interesting to see how far courses can be modified to accommodate the substantial increase in time suggested for the study of the teaching of reading. I would like to identify one particular concern which the Report may have unwittingly created, that is that language studies have become so complex that many general practitioner teachers will abdicate their responsibility to specialists.

Language teaching remains central to the whole learning process and is, therefore, the responsibility of every teacher in our schools, regardless of the age range they teach or the particular specialisms they represent. This I believe is the essential lesson to be learned from the Bullock Report.

CONCLUSION

Chapter 23 of the Report is the one concerned with initial training and it acknowledges the fact that the Report has emerged at a critical and uncertain time in the development of teacher training. One is reluctant to criticize colleagues at a time when drastic cuts are being made in student intakes and when many tutors' posts are at risk.

However, one cannot disregard what the Report refers to as the recurring theme in the evidence they gathered which stated that 'Colleges of education give too little attention to language in general and reading in particular'.

This broad generalization is followed by the following observations:

In some colleges there is still surprisingly slight attention given to the teaching of reading with students receiving little more than a few lectures of an hour's duration. More common than this extreme is the practice of a good introduction in the first year of the course but no subsequent development. Many students have, therefore, lost both knowledge and confidence by the end of their third year when they are about to start their teaching life. Furthermore, there is often an uncertain relationship between theory and practice.

These are the shortcomings brought most insistently to our attention and they are common enough to be presented as qualified generalizations. Two principal conclusions emerge from the evidence and from our discussions and visits. First, there is a remarkably wide variation in the importance attached to reading and language development in different institutions. Secondly, colleges find it difficult to provide enough time to deal adequately with these aspects in the face of the conflicting claims of other elements of professional training. Priority often goes to psychology, sociology and child development.

I have not mentioned block teaching-practice in this paper, that is the long period of practice students undertake in each year of the course. Normally this lasts not less than six weeks and in many colleges a whole term. However, I would like to draw attention to the comment on p. 340 of the Report which states, 'the language work must be given specific focus on teaching practice and this means knowledge and involvement on the part of the tutors and supervisors'.

To sum up, I consider the Report's summary of conclusions and recommendations on initial training to be wholly relevant and worthy of the most serious consideration by all concerned.

It seems to me pertinent and encouraging that the dialogue on these issues has not been confined to British institutions. Colleagues on both sides of the Atlantic have much to learn from each other.

REFERENCES

DES (1975) *A Language for Life* (Bullock Report) London: Her Majesty's Stationery Office

Teaching for communication competence

Donald H. Ecroyd

Communication is concerned with the making of choices. Those who practise it know that their proper focus must always be: 'What can *I* say to *these people* on *this topic, here and now.*' In some eras the emphasis in instruction has been on the speaker – the *I*. In others, it has been on the *topic* or message. Now it is perhaps most clearly focused on the audience – *these people.* There can be no question, however, but that the entire admonition must be considered by the teacher who has serious concern for the developing of communication competence in children.

Communication choices are varied, but always interlocking. Which role does the speaker choose to play? Which ideas will he or she present? How will those ideas be phrased to make others malleable to the speaker's purpose – interested in the speaker's words? Constantly, in oral communication whether formal or casual, we are making such choices as these, and they are made synchronically with utterance itself. Speaking, in other words, is not a linear process, but a concurrent one. Concurrently, the speaker both *has* and *encodes* ideas; and, in turn – almost simultaneously with these processes – he or she speaks. The entire object is to secure some sort of previously determined, planned-for reaction from some listener.

It is true that one sometimes speaks on impulse. There is, however, no rhetorical rule for the encoding of blue passages when you hit your thumb with a hammer. Nor is there any set of formulae appropriate for instruction on how best to gasp when first glimpsing Niagara or the Grand Canyon. By extension, no true lover ever wrote out all his lines, and no true patriot or religious zealot ever needed more than the inspiration of the moment to speak. That the man and the moment have met is enough.

When communication is encoded purposefully, however, choices do have to be made. The difficulty with isolating and defining such choice mechanisms is that they always grow out of particular situations. The pragmatics of setting govern what will be said, how it will be said, and even whether or not it will be said at all. The questions to which this paper is addressed, then, are:

1 What does the teacher do who would encourage the development of communication competence in students?
2 How do we train a teacher to do these things?

Communication strategies must not be thought of as some all-inclusive, abstract set of rules, methods, and principles. Such thinking is precisely the weakness of the Dale Carnegie kind of speech instruction. Here the transaction of speaking between people is viewed as some sort of *Monopoly* game in which you do not pass GO and do not collect $200 if you break any of the magic rules. The real objectives are to be upwardly mobile and to be able to make more money. Just follow the rules and you'll get somewhere!

Such an approach violates the essence of interactive communication as I understand it. If one's effectiveness is to be judged by how well one follows the rules of stance, eye contact and didactic outlining, any kind of process-orientation becomes a moot impossibility. If communication learning is concerned with the development and testing of coping strategies, implementing strategies and evaluating strategies, it cannot be reduced to a series of rules designed to render the making of choices unnecessary or automatic. If all one needs to do is follow the rules, there is no place in the study of language and communication for the exercise of one's own humanity. He or she need not search inward for guidance nor upward for inspiration. All that matters is outward conformity to the expectations outlined by the rules.

The question before us, as I see it, concerns what kinds of choices we think people should be able to make with regard to communication generally; and how we can go about helping school children to learn what they will probably need to know in order to make such choices in ways that will be satisfying to them as human beings, as well as useful to society.

The choices we are talking about must be left at least in part to the moment of interaction. Commonsense, a stance of impartiality, and even an aware, unabashed openness to wonder must all be somehow part of the act of communication. In such a frame of reference, the effort to understand the communicative act takes on affective as well as cognitive overtones. In addition, communication *is* a process. Its choices are designed to elicit meanings – and meanings are in people rather than in words. Communication must be an open, symbolic interaction. The literature of language learning clearly points out that the sort of communication choices we are discussing are a species-specific phenomenon known only to humans; and that our ability to make such choices is a socially-motivated development of an inborn propensity. It is true, of course, that we fulfil this propensity varyingly; but the resulting differences do not necessarily constitute deficiencies in communication ability.

Given the new psycholinguistic and sociolinguistic insights, and given the analogy of communication as a feedback-interaction model, and attending to various admonitions against mechanistic sterility, we must ask ourselves, 'What kind of instructional programme in the area of communication education should be developed in America's elementary and secondary schools?'

If this were the early 1950s instead of the late 1970s, at this point we would resolve ourselves into a committee to develop a course of study. I participated in a Governor's Committee to write a statewide course of study and decide upon a panel of textbooks for statewide adoption as recently as 1956. Today, however – in the United States at least – we have been much influenced by two important publications, and we no longer would make such an approach. The first of these documents is the *Taxonomy of Educational Objectives*, under the general editorship of Dr Benjamin Bloom (1956). The *Handbook* dealing with the cognitive domain was published in 1956, and the one dealing with the affective domain, edited by Dr David Krathwohl, was published in 1964. The second of these important publications is the programmed instructional booklet on *Preparing In-structional Objectives* written by Dr Robert Mager (1962). These publications mark the move from the artist-teacher whose concern was primarily, 'What shall I do in class?' to the scientist-teacher who asks, 'What behaviours do I want my students to be able to exhibit at the end of our time together in the classroom?'

With these new tools for analysis of curriculum and course planning, we need no longer rely exclusively upon the intuitive traditions of 'what should be taught'. Moreover, we can now do a more specific and responsible job of evaluating actual changes in pupil behaviour than we have ever managed to do in the past. I once heard James Cass, the editor of *Saturday Review*, speaking at a conference of Title III Project Directors in Washington, and his description of education prior to these new approaches has stuck in my mind. He called it education 'beautifully preparing our children to live in the generation that has just passed'.

What, then, does the *Taxonomy* do? Let us just consider the outline of the cognitive domain that Dr Bloom and his associates have given us. The lowest level of the total hierarchy of what one can learn is the level of recall knowledge. The names of things, the steps in a process in order, the recollection of pieces of factual information – these represent a very low level of cognitive learning; but a level necessary to the development of any more complex understandings. Once these bits of data are learned, there begins to develop a certain amount of comprehension – the second level of the hierarchy itself. By comprehension is meant the ability to see relationships between pieces of information, the ability to line up cause and effect sequences, to spot similarities and differences, and to tie concepts and facts together in categories. Once one has developed a certain amount of comprehension, the level of application becomes open; and once one is consciously applying comprehension of knowledge to actual situations, it becomes possible to analyse what one is doing – to isolate factors for comment and to see part functions both as elemental entities and as related to the broader wholes which they help make up. Once one has developed a storehouse of knowledge, has a certain amount of comprehension, has applied his learning, and has attempted analysis, it becomes possible to move the more complex level of synthesis and the most sophisticated level of all – evaluation. The teacher who uses this analytical scheme to plan what he or she wants pupils to learn, will not make the mistake of structuring the class for application and synthesis, then testing for knowledge and comprehension. Neither will that teacher be likely to move into evaluation-level discussions without first checking on the class ability to apply concepts and analyse them.

Mager's approach suggests that we must chart the terminal behaviours we seek in our students, and train them with these behaviours as a goal. In other words, one does not organize a course by outlining chapters in the text for discussion, or by setting up a series of speaking or writing assignments. Such matters are not properly 'objectives' at all, but merely particular materials or performance tasks. The first order of business is to establish objectives in terms of the outcome behaviours you want from your students. Once these are clear to you, you can devise strategies for reaching them; choose particular materials and methods for fulfilling those strategies; and determine your means of evaluating for pupil mastery of the objectives you originally specified. The behaviours identified will fall somewhere into the structure of the taxonomy, depending upon one or more of the following:

1   The teacher's conception of what should be taught.
2   The place of the training-goals decided upon in the total course structure of the school.
3   The individual needs and goals of the pupil.
4   The practical time limits available for instruction.
5   The motivation level of the teacher, the students and the administration.
6   The cooperation and reinforcement level of the general community and the school administration.

The elementary-school child arrives in the classroom with a working knowledge of language and a working repertory of communication strategies. Although scholars are not in complete agreement, it seems generally true that, at certain age levels, the child's innate propensity to language is capable of expansion in definable directions. For example, if there is to be any generalized classroom approach to the development of a stable phonology, it clearly must occur in the preschool and first grade. By the age of seven and a half even the most conservative of experts would agree that the phonological system is frozen, and that new sound production schemes are only going to be learned after much expenditure of effort and energy. The syntactic competence seems to be largely set by the age of six, but some of the more complex and sophisticated structures are probably not complete until the age of nine, ten or eleven. Semantic learning – the relating of symbol to reality – seems to continue through adolescence for most of us; perhaps even up to the age of eighteen. In other words, the teacher in grades two to six can be working with the movables of language, helping pupils find an ever wider repertory of expression. This teacher can be helping students through experiences requiring the expression of tentative judgments, the expression of alternatives, and the use of what Bernstein calls the elaborated code (Bernstein (1964)). Once the pupil arrives in junior high school, however, the teacher's attention should focus upon the paralinguistic tasks of expressing role, mood, meaning; for the only linguistic development still going on is at the level of vocabulary growth.

Most teachers will readily agree that we should be teaching for an awareness in the child of the language structures which he or she has already learned. All too often, however, we rather quickly degenerate into a discussion of 'correct and incorrect' usage. This sort of approach has a way of turning off the valuing of the intimate, personal ideolect until – in adults – it all too often ends up being the exclusive property of poets. Instead of structuring our class time so that our pupils may learn the wonder, the stance of objectivity, or even the commonsense that group interaction can uniquely teach, we insist upon 'holding up your hand', 'speaking in complete sentences', and 'standing while you answer the question'. If the child brings a social dialect into the classroom which is noticeably different from the social dialect of the teacher, the process becomes even more complicated in many cases by the teacher's insistence upon the student's using a different pattern of speech from that in which his or her ideas would ordinarily be expressed.

Most teachers will readily agree that we should be teaching for an expansion of the child's already-present language, and most will recognize that one of the best ways of doing this is by broadening the experience horizon of the child. Thus field trips are taken, stories are read and records are played. Then opportunities are set up in which the child can 'play out' roles from the stories, or from the special experiences which were developed and planned for the class. However, once the story hour is over and the last role has been played, in too many classes number skills, social studies, art, music, and even recreational games are then taught as if the language arts experiences had occurred on another planet, or in another time-zone. In the language arts period the children are encouraged to talk together, and to work out group solutions to problems. In arithmetic, everyone must stay completely silent and to confer verges upon being a criminal act.

Most teachers will readily agree that we should be teaching for a valuing of language, and trying to develop in our pupils a sense of comfortableness in its use. Yet in all too many classrooms, the student is never asked a question that cannot be answered with 'yes', 'no', or the name of something. If a pupil were to respond to a question by saying, 'That's a good question. I'd like to think it over' he would probably be sent to the Principal's office and labelled as some sort of smart-alec.

Minimally, our goals for the teaching of communication should include the following:

1 The speech and listening abilities of the child should be appropriate to his or her own age level, and to the language community from which the child comes.
2 This core of language should be expanded by the school in ways related to the natural development of language competence. Either the strategies of pattern-practice drill (Skinnerian behaviour-modification techniques), or strategies based upon creative experience (cognitive growth) may be used, depending upon which is the more appropriate to the learning task.
3 The expansion of language should be carried out in the total school programme, and should be made both relevant and fun. 'Oracy', in other words, should not only be taught in ways that increase verbal ability, but also in ways that increase the

child's joy in communicating, and broaden his or her perceptions of the total process.

In order to move towards these broad goals, we need to specify particular behaviours for attention, and devise strategies for bringing about change. We cannot trust to unstructured procedures, for such procedures do not lead to measurable results. We should avoid prescription and instead observe the present usage of each pupil, deriving theory from that usage and then developing teaching strategies that will permit the application and practice of the theories we have derived. For example, in an inner-city class, we may find it highly desirable to teach the child to read the dialect he speaks without 'correction' before teaching him anything about 'classroom speech' or Standard English. With the Spanish-speaking youngster, it may be highly desirable to permit instruction in Spanish for a while, perhaps even insisting that English-speaking children in the same classroom learn some Spanish while the others are learning their English. In this way we can derive our theory of choices from the practice before us – not from some normative abstraction which may be singularly inappropriate for the needs and motivations of the children we are working with.

Even in the lower grades we must carefully avoid the kind of communication instruction that equates 'rule following' with communication effectiveness. Simply because the teacher makes an oral assignment does not mean that the student will have a learning experience in oral communication. As famed American speech teacher and scholar, James M. O'Neil, observed frequently, 'A speech is not an essay on its hind legs'. Effective oral interaction cannot be thought of as being the same thing as reading off a report; nor does learning to 'take turns' constitute any vital understanding of the art of group discussion. The teacher who has students play little elocution games probably teaches them very little that is positive or helpful about communication. One sure way to teach students how to avoid breaking any of the rules is to insist that they speak from memory. One sure way to teach that speech communication is not a very important skill is to have a lot of little impromptu talks in class on silly or trivial subjects. One sure way to teach that communication is not a process is to have students 'write a speech' on such-and-such, which may or may not ever be given. The result of such approaches is not communication at all, but a game in which the byword is 'wake me up when it's my turn'. Such approaches negate the essence of communication. No interaction except with the teacher is possible. The object of the game – and it is a very stupid, dull game – is to avoid violating any rules in some sort of repetitive 'show and tell in Standard English'. The one who wins will be rewarded: embarrassment comes for the loser.

The focus, I believe, should be upon the listener, not on the self. The focus should be on the behaviour of the one who hears, not merely upon the behaviour of the one who speaks. Speech requires a sense of interaction – a constant awareness of the listener and the situation. This kind of objectivity and common-sense cannot be taught by elocutionary methods which focus upon the speaker, nor can they be taught by English composition methods which focus upon the message. If we are to help our students learn to make effective communication choices, we must teach them first to observe their own practices; then help them derive theory from that observation, and finally give them opportunities to practise the theory they have derived.

American researchers in the field of speech are in general agreement that listening, speaking, reading and writing are integrally related. Unless one has heard particular words or usages, one is not likely to speak them. Similarly, whatever is a part of the speaking/listening vocabulary will be readable, and if readable, it will be capable of being written. These skills, however, are not best taught in some sort of isolation unless there is a clinically definable problem. As the Bullock Report states, 'Reading, writing, talking and listening are associated abilities which should go on developing throughout a pupil's educational life' (p. 26). American authorities also generally agree with the Report when it suggests:

1 All learning evolves from discovery.
2 Language has an heuristic function – in all four of its aspects.
3 'To exploit the process of discovery through language in all its uses is the surest means of enabling a child to master his mother tongue.' (p.50)

American speech communication scholars also warm to the Report's urging of planned intervention techniques (p. 67) and the clear feeling that every teacher teaches some aspect of language (p. 146). The result of these shared understandings is a shared feeling that all teachers should be carefully trained in goals of communication instruction. As Barbara Wood (1976) writes in *Children and Communication: Verbal and Nonverbal Language Development*:

The primary goal of communication instruction is to increase the child's repertoire of communication strategies in critical communication situations. The secondary goal is this: children will participate in a greater variety of communication situations if they feel confident that they can communicate appropriately. The instructional model contains two components. The major component reflects the parameters of communication in critical situations. Situations are defined by the four parameters of participants, setting, topic and task. The second component includes the range of communication strategies employed by children in these communication situations. Communication strategies include the use of both verbal and nonverbal choices.

In an effort to determine what such communication choices and strategies might be, the Speech Communication Association called a national conference on the training of teachers of oral communication for Memphis in the summer of 1972. (See the report of this conference *New Horizons* R. R. Allen and P. Judson Newcombe 1973.) Following this conference, the Speech Communication Association sponsored a national project on speech communication competencies, funded by the Axe-Houghton Foundation. The report of this project (R. R. Allen and Kenneth Brown 1976) suggests first of all that the teaching of communication strategies cannot be profitably undertaken as a result of direct instruction; but that the teacher must instead structure experiences from which the strategies can be learned. In an article published in 1973, I offered four generalizations about the role of the teacher in encouraging speech and language learning. These still seem relevant to our consideration:

1 The teacher is an important language model in the student's world.
2 The teacher is a primary source of language reinforcement and feedback.
3 The teacher shapes the roles students play in the classroom – perhaps in life.
4 The teacher teaches information and skill about the communication process, whether deliberately and consciously or not.

As my graduate students put in our chapter in *Developing Communication Competence in Children* (Allen and Brown 1976), 'Whether or not we can actually teach communication is perhaps moot, but there seems to be no question concerning our ability to model desirable communication behaviours, reinforce them and offer feedback, shape roles, and structure experiences in which learning can occur.'

In the development of the two TRIPS (Theory and Research into Practice) booklets commissioned through the Speech Communication Association by ERIC (Wood *et al.* 1977), the aspect of structuring experiences in which communication learning can occur is given special attention. Assuming, first of all, that communication strategies are learned from experiences involving communication acts, the TRIPS authors look to the Speech Communication Association national project results for guidance, and define such acts as: controlling, feeling, informing, ritualizing and imagining. Controlling speech acts are communications in which the communicator seeks to control the behaviour of others. Communication acts in which the principal aim is to express or respond to feelings and attitudes are a part of the second category. Informing communication acts include explaining, questioning, justifying, naming, demonstrating, defining, and the like. Ritualizing acts may be formal – as in reciting, greeting, leave-taking, thanking; but may also be informal – as in participating in verbal games or shocking. Imagining communicative acts include creative behaviours such as fantasizing, role-playing, speculating, theorising, and storytelling. Communication strategies in each area of 'act' include implementing strategies, coping strategies and evaluating strategies: 'Competence refers to a person's knowledge of how to use language appropriately in all kinds of communication situations' (*Grades 7-12* booklet).

What the teacher in training would be taught, then, would consist of:

1 Knowledge and comprehension of patterns of language and communication learning (code learning, communication roles and norms, the affective component, etc).
2 Identification of structures for planning learning experiences (the Bloom and Krathwohl taxonomies, behavioural objectives, criterion reference testing and evaluation, etc).
3 Concepts and values related to the nature of 'communication acts', and selection criteria for appropriateness relevant for each age group.
4 Ranges of implementing choices, and evaluative repertories of criteria, appropriate to communication learning and performance at each age level.

Communication instruction is the common concern of all teachers, and the programme of communication instruction should therefore be an integrated and total one. The instructional environment should be experiential – one which promotes rather than constrains student communication and involvement.

To sum up, then, I believe first of all that theory must be thought of as a means of opening up choices. The student must learn to value communication as a process; and we, his or her teachers, must learn in turn to value the skill that the student brings into our classroom. What we should be about is the development of 'oracy'—the speaking and listening components of communication skill. Upon the level of such oracy depends literacy – especially in the first six grades where the reading and speaking vocabularies always overlap. Upon the level of oracy also depends so much of what we can tell about language competency, that through language expansion generally, in all probabilities, we do the most to develop that internal, elusive process of thought. In addition, we must think behaviourally. First, then, we should urge teachers in training to become scientist-teachers. We should teach them to concentrate upon the behaviours they want their pupils to be able to exhibit, then experiment with a variety of strategies to achieve them. Communication is the most human of all human acts, and your teaching should be – yes, must be – designed to give it effectiveness.

REFERENCES

ALLEN, R. R. and JUDSON NEWCOMBE, P. (1973) (Eds) *New Horizons* Skokie, Illinois: National Textbook Company

ALLEN, R. R. and BROWN, K. (1976) (Eds) *Developing Communication Competencies in Children* Skokie, Illinois: National Textbook Company

BERNSTEIN, B. (1964) 'Elaborated and restricted codes: their social origins and some consequences' in J. Gumperz and D. Hymes (Eds) *The Ethnography of Communication* special publication of the *American Anthropologist* 66:6, 2, pp. 55–59

BLOOM, B. *et al.* (1956) *Taxonomy of Educational Objectives, Handbook 1; Cognitive Domain* New York: David McKay

BLOOM, B. *et al.* (1964) *Taxonomy of Educational Objectives, Handbook 2: Affective Domain* New York: David McKay

ECROYD, D. (1973) The relevance of oral language development to classroom teaching *Today's Speech* 21, pp. 15–16

JACOBSON, B., LARDNER, G., MORAN, J., RONNEY, R., ECROYD, D. 'The affective component of communication development' in R. R. Allen and K. Brown (Eds) *Developing Communication Competence in Children* Skokie, Illinois: National Textbook Company

MAGER, R. (1962) *Preparing Instructional Objectives* Belmont, California: Fearon

WOOD, B. (1976) *Children and Communication: Verbal and Nonverbal Language Development* Englewood Cliffs, New Jersey: Prentice-Hall

WOOD, B., BROWN, K., ECROYD, D., HOPPER, R. (1977) *Developing Communicative Competence in Children: Grades K-6; Developing Communicative Competence in Children: Grades 7-12* TRIPS (Theory and Research Into Practice) Booklets, available through NCTE or SCA

5 Language issues and policies: inside some British schools

INTRODUCTION

The articles in this section are concerned with the impact of the Bullock Report on language and literacy teaching in British infant, junior and comprehensive secondary schools. Each attempts to describe the general climate of thought and practice which existed at the time of the Report's publication, and since. By implication, each author contends that the existing climate has, to a great extent, shaped the way in which both individual schools and local authorities have responded to the Report's various recommendations, particularly the one regarding 'language across the curriculum'.

Frances Davis provides an optimistic view of the Report's reception by teachers in modern infant schools. By 1975, school staffs in many parts of the country were already working energetically on developing more enlightened and more soundly integrated language programmes for their children. Some staffs, in fact, were working explicitly on preparing language policies, not as fixed documents but as flexible, constantly evolving and changing statements which would provide guidance for all teachers in those schools. In such a context, the Bullock Report was warmly received and used to inform, document and extend discussions of literacy teaching that were already underway.

F. J. G. Poole discusses Bullock's relevance for junior schools in light of the Plowden Report and its effects and countereffects. Primary-school teachers, he argues, had been stung by recent criticisms of progressive methods and were ready to turn to the Bullock Report for solid guidance in examining their work and in bringing 'the whole question of language teaching into focus'. These discussions are well underway now, both within and among schools, and it is Poole's view that they will give rise to sounder, more positive and more unified approaches to language and literacy teaching across the entire country.

Ramin Minovi's view of the impact of the Bullock Report in comprehensive schools is much less optimistic. On the whole, as he claims, teachers in comprehensive schools do not read new research or new discussions of teaching practice, nor are they accustomed to discussing issues of language learning across departmental lines. Thus, for example, responses to Bullock's recommendations that school staffs develop policies for language across the curriculum have come from local authorities, not teachers themselves, and the teachers who have participated in such discussions often come to them thinking narrowly that they would be discussing a new teaching method. Perhaps Manovi is wrong, but once again it seems a national report on educational practice in British schools will be considered and implemented most enthusiastically and knowledgeably by teachers of younger children. Some secondary-school teachers will also consider the Report seriously and implement its recommendations thoughtfully. Will it ever happen in England or America, though, that teachers of both younger and older children, together, examine their own teaching practices in the light of such a sound and impressive national report?

Language policies in modern British infant schools

Frances R. A. Davis

British children usually attend infant school between the ages of five and seven years. These are crucial years for literacy development and teachers of children of this age usually are aware of their responsibilities in helping children learn to organize and express their thoughts in speech and writing. How these responsibilities are discharged, however, is frequently a matter of considerable concern to those responsible for children's education. This concern often embroils teachers and parents in controversy about methods of instruction.

During their observation of infant schools, the Bullock Committee found, in varying degrees, that some schools employed very traditional methods and others were clearly progressive. While the Committee wisely avoided the disagreements surrounding methods and concentrated on literacy issues across the spectrum of all types of schools, this paper focuses on the more informal infant school. The changes towards informality profoundly affected the language-teaching policies of these schools; it was the informal infant school which responded most fully to, and in some cases was a forerunner of, the philosophical intent of the Report.

THE VALUE OF BULLOCK FOR BRITISH INFANT TEACHERS
The Bullock Committee's recommendations for infant language learning helped school staffs look more objectively at the learning environments they provide for children. The Committee's Report and its subsequent discussion aided teachers in assessing themselves the strengths and weaknesses of their literacy programmes – not according to some particular and static standard, but in view of what individual children actually were doing in their classes.

The Report's publication also provided teachers with an overall perspective of literacy teaching. Because of the underlying philosophy and organization reflected by the Report, infant teachers could see their role more clearly in the continuum of language learning throughout the life span. The infant teachers could see their responsibility for language learning as encompassing the issues of language from home to school and from infant school to the junior school. The web of living and language learning in the school could be considered more fully in relation to the context of lifetime literacy development.

LITERACY AND THE CONTEXT OF THE INFANT SCHOOL

What comprises the web of infant school classrooms? The 'modern' infant school is not defined simply by open construction or special age groupings. The contextual parts of the modern infant classroom do not depend upon a particular instructional method, configuration or appearance of the classroom. The infant school may be some, or all, of the concepts one considers as part of an informal learning situation; but beyond these the classrooms provoke a particular feeling, a woven sense of real living, understanding and concern for the individuality of children and their language.

A headmistress who told me of her return to teaching following the second world war expresses this sense of living in the life of the infant school. She said that on her return to London from evacuation with her two children she decided to return to teaching. When she walked into the infant school and saw the children confined to desks, mutely following drill instructions, she knew changes had to be made in the school and its policies. The picture she gives of those older schools sharply contrasts with the reality of her school today. First housed in a building constructed during the 1800s, the younger children of the school moved to a new building during the 1960s, and the whole school was unified at the new location in 1976 with the addition of temporary classrooms. Even in the days when the older infants were physically located in the old building, the antiquated facility made only a slight difference in the programme developed for the children. The leadership of the headmistress and the quality of the staff encouraged a feeling of shared purpose, of the individuality and worth of children; the humane treatment of all within the school.

The atmosphere of the infant school is considered by staffs and heads as a most important aspect of its 'web of living'. This comes, in part, from their feeling that the school extends, not replaces, the home. One inner-London school I frequently visit has developed changes in the school as the intake area around the school has changed. Formerly an affluent middle-class area with double flats and single houses, huge 'blocks' were built to provide housing for large numbers of people. With these high-rise apartments came many children who lacked space to develop play activities. The multidwelling buildings also tended to insulate families so that children experienced little social play before school. Pets were uncommon in the buildings, and television inappropriately used as a child-minding device. With the changes that occurred in the intake area, the staff saw a rise in emotional difficulties as well as a variety of language-learning problems. These children exhibited the inevitable learning and behaviour patterns that such problems usually bring. The increase in the number of bilingual children required specialized language instruction.

The staff of the school responded to the multiplicity of problems related to the changes in the composition of their intake area and made adjustments in their language programme. They provided specialized work for the bilingual and language-restricted children, and mobilized school resources to cope with children exhibiting emotional difficulties. Some further changes were: providing social and play experiences for children to help them build relationships among themselves; remedial work for those unable to benefit from the regular programme; the addition of a male teacher to the staff to serve as a model for some children; arrangement for outside clinical help as needed; and increased attention to the music and arts programmes. The staff also made sure that school pets were available to the children. Never have I visited this school when a special school dog was not present. Some years the dog belonged to the headmistress and came with her each day; other years someone on the staff brought a dog regularly to school.

In the process of evolving plans to meet the problems in their school, this inner-London school staff realized the need for a policy of language learning and teaching for all of the children. Eventually the policy which the staff established became a written plan which tended to unify the teachers' purposes in teaching literacy. The policy is not static; it is fluid and ever changing. In defining their goals and writing the policy, teachers were able to see where they stood in teaching language, and where they might hope to be on such learning-teaching issues as oral language, pre-reading, early reading, writing, spelling, phonics, materials for teaching reading and progress records. The study and examinations of existing practices in their school, and its reflection of constant change, is exactly what the Bullock Committee recommended. The establishment of a flexible policy allowed for continued observation of the learning situation, identification of problem areas, and extension of the policies to meet those problems.

Language, learning, and the integrated day
Bullock recommended the use of language as a tool for learning. To the Committee the uses of language for talking and writing were equally as important as its uses for reading and listening. Does this attitude have any relationship to the combining of disciplines which the modern infant school organizes into a plan for an integrated day? Regardless of grouping practices – that is, family grouping where children are of mixed ages or grouping by chronological age – most modern infant schools base their instruction on a format known as the integrated day. Weber (1971) describes this in her book, *English Infant School and Informal Education*, as a free day:

> In planning for the free day there is no separation of activities or skills and no separate scheduling of any one activity other than the fixed points (morning service, PE, music and movement, and lunch) designed for all the children in the school. As a result, one might see all aspects of the environment – reading, writing, number, painting, acting, music – in use at all

times. A group getting the teacher's special help or stimulus could be found at any time.

Does this type of instruction fit in with Bullock's recommendations? As I indicated earlier in this paper, the Committee was careful not to seem to make specific suggestions about methods; in fact, it commented that their work was much more difficult because the discussion of language matters frequently led to a discussion of method. They were moved to say, however, that the extreme views of formal or informal proponents were not helpful: 'It seems to us unfortunate that public debate has tended in recent years to oversimplify a complex situation and has often been conducted through a series of slogan-like headings: progressive, formal, integration, basics, and several more' (p. 199). While it is true that the integrated day carried to an extreme could lead to a lowering of standards; it could, when used constructively, provide more opportunity for children to use and explore language on their own under the guidance of an alert teacher. What actually does happen in most integrated-day classrooms in infant schools? A general answer to this question is not available, but two boys in the same inner-London school I described earlier may provide a partial answer. Their activities also illustrate the attitude of the staff towards relationships between language and learning.

In a 'rising-seven' classroom, I observed two boys busily writing and manipulating a set of about ten 100 × 100 mm blue cards. One boy was writing numerals on one side of each card and the other was writing something on the other side of the cards. There was much talk between them as to what should be written – if that was the right thing to write on that particular card, and so forth. The boys argued, then decided, then discussed their problem again. As they worked they exchanged ideas and sometimes cards. 'You do five, I'll do six,' they agreed, and then changed their minds about who was doing what. When I asked them what they were doing, they said, 'Directions – we're taking it down to pres to show what we've done.' When I was puzzled and asked what 'pres' was, they said, 'You know, pres – down there,' and they pointed out of the window, across the terrace to a building on a level below where we were sitting. Completely mystified, I said, 'Down where?' Very exasperated with this visitor who found their accent difficult to understand, they answered, '*You* know, down there, down in the hole,' and they continued to point down the slope between the buildings. I looked at the cards for some clue as to what it was they were doing. They were numbered on one side and had directions written on the other:

Card 1 Get your bricks.
Card 2 Make a wall 81 cm, 87 cm, 73 cm, 89 cm, 28 cm.
Card 3 Make a roof.
Card 4 We put bricks too hold it up.
(Cards 5 and 6 were unfinished, but it was clear the boys planned to continue to about 10 cards.)

Still at a loss about what the boys were doing, I asked their teacher, a student from the Froebel Institute under the direction of the classroom teacher. She translated 'pres' as prayers and 'hole' as hall for me. The hall is both a place and an event in the boys' school life. It is used for movement activities with gymnastics apparatus, music, lunch and the daily morning all-school meeting which is called 'Prayers' by the children. This daily meeting is the only government-specified infant school activity (Education Act of 1944) and takes place each morning shortly after the school day starts. Music by piano or record usually is played as class by class files by to sit in groups upon the floor. The children sing *God Save the Queen* and listen attentively as they are greeted by the headmistress, receive the day's instructions and participate in the programme in various ways. The programme varies, sometimes a bit of poetry is read, children sing songs, or play instruments, and classes share their work with the entire school. The two boys in the 'rising-seven' classroom who were working with the blue cards were preparing their project to take to the Friday morning prayer session in the hall.

How did their project come about? For some time the teacher noticed the two boys building forts out on the terrace. She encouraged them to make a plan of the fort, which they did by rebuilding one on a large sheet of paper and tracing around it. At the time I observed them, they had carried their project to the point of making a list of provisions that would be needed should they be besieged in the fort. Their 'blockade list' included such practical items as tea and sausages. The blue cards on which they were writing when I saw them contained directions for anyone who wanted to build another fort just like the one they built. This is the kind of language learning that Bullock suggests for young children. From a self-initiated activity, the teacher guided the boys into a project which involved problem-solving through talking about the problem, measuring, numbering, sequencing, writing, spelling, reading, planning, and presenting. This is language in action; it was derived from the action of the boys.

Systematic instruction in reading

The boys' project with the fort is the kind of learning that is happening in many infant schools, but the language effort is not limited to that type of learning. Systematic and individualized instruction is also provided. Sometimes this occurs in large or small groups, and often it takes place with one child working alone or with an adult. Around the room where the two boys were working on their blue cards, homemade cloth pockets hung on walls and room-dividers. Each pocket held one child's reading materials – a reading book in which there was a marker – as well as a selection of other books. The page the child last read was noted on the marker, the words he found difficult, and the point at which he should begin the next time someone listened to him read. Children approached me with their books, and with the teacher's permission we reviewed the difficult words and went on reading new material. I made the notations for the next reading session.

The description of the boys' project with the fort and of the provisions made for individualized reading are examples of this inner-London infant school's written language policy in action. The school also has included in its policy a unified approach across classes in getting children ready to read. The effort here is consonant with the Bullock recommendations which adopt our contemporary view of readiness:

It cannot be emphasized too strongly that the teacher has to help the children towards readiness for beginning to read.

There is no question of waiting for readiness to occur; for with many children it does not come 'naturally' and must be brought about by the teacher's positive measure to induce it. (p. 102)

This view avoids simply waiting for the child to mature to a point of readiness and stresses actively aiding the child to become ready. The teachers in this inner-London school know that when children enter their classes they come with many different personalities as well as abilities. The teacher must help them develop emotional maturity and stability which in turn will affect confidence, effort and concentration. These in turn affect the child's ability to deal with the growing demands of symbolization. Oral language is strengthened, sensory and motor skills practised, and motivation is developed by encouraging children to become interested in reading. When formal reading instruction is provided, it is not limited to one method of teaching, but an integrated, flexible approach is built on a variety of materials and experiences of the children.

The process of writing development
The writing the children do in the infant school should be thought of as a compositional activity rather than simply an exercise in writing skill. Writing, built on the personal experiences of the children, is both a writing and a reading experience. All writing in the infant school is meant for reading whether it is in the labels teachers provide for places and objects in the room; group-experience stories children compose which the teacher writes; or the writing of individual children.

Since 1972 I have studied the development of storytelling and writing in British and American schools. During my visits to Britain, many children wrote stores for me and read to me the stories they wrote for their regular class work. These are most often stories based on their own or vicarious experiences, and the process of learning to write them on paper is common to most infant schools. It is a composing-writing process which takes place on three progressive levels. First, the child dictates to an adult who writes the words on paper. A second part of this first level occurs when the child begins to trace over the teacher's printing. The second level develops as greater motor control and coordination is achieved and the child copies the teacher's printing underneath the words. A third level occurs when the child begins to write independently. At this level it is usual to see the child organizing a personal dictionary of words to use for writing. While most of the children's writing is based on personal experiences, the more advanced children begin to consult outside sources as a background for their writing. I observed a particularly good example of this three-level process in a family-grouped classroom in a rural village school. The children's writings were all based upon their class trip to see the Outwood Windmill. Copies of their writings are reproduced below, complete with the original spellings (Davis 1977)

1 *(Adult printed, child copied below)*
   I went to have a picnic at the windmill.
   Charles, age 4
2 *(Adult printed, child copied below)*
   This is my windmill. The sails are turning.
   Jonothan, age 5
3 *(Independent writing)*
   May 3rd
   On Thursday I went to see the old mill we went inside the mill I saw big wheels go round.
   Richard, age 5
4 *(Independent writing)*
   The story of Outwood Mill
   On Thursday we went on an outing to outwood mill. It was great fun. It was built in 1665. It is very old. I was in Mrs Mitchells group. She is nice. It is 38 fee talle. The sails are 59 inches long.
   Deborah, age 6
5 *(Independent writing)*
   The story of outwood mill.
   On Thursday we went on an outing and when we got there we got out of the coach and then we had afood around and then hey askes us when was outwood mill built and it was built in 1665, and just 1 year ahead in 1666 they saw the great fire of London.

Giles, age 6

6 (*Independent writing*)
The story of outwood mill
The mill of outwood was built in 1665. When the men were building they looked over to London and saw smoke rising to the sky. It was the fire of London and finis the roof off, and then it came to 1974 when Mrs Brights and Mrs Dellers went we found out how long the sales were they were 59 inches long. We found out how high it was. It was 39 feet high.

Lisa, age 7

7 (*Independent writing*)
June 7th
The History of Windmills
Mills were invented by Arabs. Early mills have wooden bodys, and have four sails. They are mounted on a stout-post to turn the mill to carach the wind. At one time there were perhaps 10,000 windmills in England but now fewer than 50 of these are left in use. There are lots of mills in Holland and Germany.

Paul, age 7

These writings illustrate the way children grow in their abilities to represent their thoughts on paper. The five year old (sample 3) has started to write independently, and the most advanced seven year old (sample 7) has reached the point of looking for outside information about the topic. In addition to illustrating the progression of the three-level writing process, and the use of children's personal experiences as a take-off point for writing, these and other stories like them provide an example of the type of instructional materials available to the children. These writings are put on posters and in books, read, reread, and cherished by the children.

Many other examples of this writing process could be given. The inner-London school room described above was filled with such writing, though all of it was at the upper levels of the process since it was a rising-seven classroom. One girl in this same room was working on a crayon drawing of a picnic scene. She wrote, independently:

This is Jellystone Park and there are children running around in the parek. There are apples are falling down.

She pointed to the bear in the picture and said, 'That's me, that's Yogi Bear.' I asked, 'Where did you hear about Yogi Bear?' 'From the telly,' she answered.

Other examples come from classrooms in a borough north of London (Davis 1973). Included in these classes were a number of 'dispersal' children from less affluent areas. These children, primarily East Indians and Pakistanis, were bused from their home district in an effort to provide them with equal educational opportunity. A display from the five year olds' reception class was set up in the hall. This writing, stimulated by a BBC broadcast, had been presented earlier in the week at morning prayer service.

1   Ducks like water. Frogs like water. These animals like water. A crocodile likes water. Fish like water. Polar bears like water.

2   These are some of the things we found out about water.
    When water freezes it makes ice.
    The ice is melting.
    When water boils it makes steam.
    When steam cools it makes water again.
    Clouds are like steam when they turn into drops of water it rains.

In a rising-seven classroom in the same school, the children showed me an experience book they and the teacher constructed with photographs and text about their trip to the post office. In the same room I received a piece of on-the-spot independent writing which was cut short because the bus arrived and because the Indian child who wrote it really had little information on which to base her writing. However, the event seemed important enough to her to record.

There is a ladea called Mrs Davis.
I am Neem.
Neem, age 6

Standards and assessment of language learning

What of standards? How much attention does the teacher give the misspellings and other errors that young children make? At the infant levels the emphasis is upon organizing thought and putting it into writing. Substance and developing skills in reading and writing are of primary importance. As children progress and become confident about their reading and writing, teachers begin in a tactful way to help them see the necessity for spelling and writing correctly. Another aid in this direction is the constant reading and rereading the children's writings receive. If the written piece cannot be read, it cannot communicate; and children soon become aware of this fact. Teachers who also are cognisant of the problems children encounter in the area of correctness provide a model through their own printing of classroom stories and notices as well as special help for the children who need it. As the Bullock Committee found, teachers are aware and concerned about both creativity and standards of literacy. Most teachers are interested in maintaining a balance between allowing thought to flow onto paper and the correctness of the writing itself.

Keeping track of student progress in reading and writing is one aspect of literacy development in the infant-school classroom which can be very time consuming – especially when one considers that many infant classes have a student–teacher ratio of thirty-to-one. Many infant teachers keep individual folders for children which show the progress the child makes in reading, language workcards, books completed; they include in this folder samples of writing and other classroom work such as mathematics and number work. Checklists of special abilities are used as well as jottings and anecdotal notes.

Many teachers, products themselves of the eleven-plus examination, are concerned and wary of standardized testing procedures. They agree with Bullock that the tests in use at the present time by national surveys are inadequate measures for assessing literacy. While infant teachers are serious in their desire to help children acquire a foundation for more mature reading and writing, they do not feel current national tests would promote this.

Gifted children

One problem area that surfaced during the discussions of the language policy at the inner-London school mentioned earlier in this paper, was that of stretching the more able children. As efforts in this school extended to meet the challenges of 'block' and immigrant children, the staff became aware that those children who found average work extremely easy lacked the everyday stimulation they needed for growth. Examination of the problem led to increased efforts to identify these children and provide them with special help. The efforts made with these children were rewarded with their outstanding progress. The addition of this area to the policy scheme in 1977 recognized an identified 'need' and provided the staff with a base for operation.

Parent relationships with the infant school

The continuity of language learning from home to school is recognized by this inner-London school and by the other infant schools I visited throughout southern England. Parents frequently walk their children to school, and they can be seen waiting outside the gate at lunchtime or at the end of the school day to walk the children home. This interest builds a relationship between the home and the school, and provides an opportunity for teachers and parents to talk with one another on an informal basis. Parents frequently help in the schools, though some schools shun parental help with reading because they feel that early reading instruction in school is an important professional responsibility for trained teachers. However, in some schools selected parents do assist in reading by coming into the classroom to hear individual children read. At other times parents aid the school by providing funds for items the school budget cannot include. School after school has its annual spring school fair, or 'disco', which raises money for items the school would not be able to acquire without additional funds. The Board of Managers, a community group which serves in a directory capacity for each school, actively works with the headmistress and staff to arrange events such as these. They are community-wide efforts, and some of the incidentals might be surprising for American visitors. One headmistress I frequently visit was slightly embarrassed when I arrived one morning and found several bottles of wine on her desk. These were door prizes which were donated by the local pub. This contribution would not likely be solicited by a public school in the United States. Whatever the parent and community support of the infant school entails, be it fund-raising through fairs or 'discos', or quasi-instructional support in the classroom, the relationships that develop between the school and parents become a positive force for children's learning.

PERSPECTIVES ON THE ROLE OF TEACHING LITERACY

The modern infant school's stand on literacy is, and is expected to be, constantly evolving. Foremost among its concerns are the issues of prereading, reading and writing instruction; variations of personal experiences on which to base language expression; teaching of children with atypical behaviour and language patterns; parent-school relationships; and standards and their evaluation. The reflection of these issues in the Bullock Report, however, juxtaposed against the Committee's stand about the role of language in learning is seen in the context of the Committee's emphasis upon literacy learning over the life span. This perspective extends the infant staff's view of their role in developing children's language processes in school. The discussions about the Report and its issues among staffs tends to help develop greater depths of understanding about literacy development.

To many teachers the ideas expressed by the Bullock Committee in relation to the early years of schooling were not new. Exhibiting a careful concern for literacy learning within the context of an environment fostering individuality, these teachers already saw a close connection between language and thought development. PreBullock, they saw language learning as encompassing all the areas of their teaching. Literacy development was, and is, to them the primary growth area for children in their classes.

The Bullock Committee's investigation of infant school literacy learning and teaching served to help infant school staffs unify their language teaching policies. The discussion of issues following the Report's release aided staffs by encouraging them to articulate their language policies for themselves and others.

For example, while not in itself a direct result of the Bullock Report, the findings and recommendations of the Committee strengthened the written language policy of the inner-London infant school described earlier in this paper. Though the written policy derived from the discussions and consensus reached by the school staff, the written policy refers specifically to the Committee's recommendations and is clearly within the philosophical framework of the Bullock Report.

REFERENCES

DAVIS, F. A. (1973) Informal Educational Practices in British Schools: Visitation Notes and Comments About Open Education (Unpublished paper)

DAVIS, F. A. (1974) A Comparative Study of British and American Seven-year-old Children's Storytelling (Unpublished paper)

DAVIS, F. A. (1977) Writing development in some British infant schools *Young Children* 32, 3

MARTIN, N. (1971) 'What are they up to?' A. Jones and J. Mulford (Eds) *Children Using Language* Oxford, England: Oxford University Press

ROSEN, C. and ROSEN, H. (1973) *The Language of Primary School Children* Harmondsworth, England: Penguin

WEBER, L. (1971) *The English Infant School and Informal Education* Englewood Cliffs, New Jersey: Prentice-Hall

The Bullock Report - its relevance to the junior school

F. J. G. Poole

For many and diverse reasons, education at all levels in Britain was in need of such a comprehensive and detailed reexamination and analysis of objectives, methods and standards related to the teaching of the English language as the Report of the Bullock Committee provides. Its findings and recommendations, while relevant to all age groups, have particular relevance to the junior school for which its influence in the period ahead will likely surpass that of the Plowden Report.

The importance of the Bullock Report lies in its comprehensive treatment of language as the essential learning tool in the whole period from birth to maturity, and its stress on continuity between schools. It will therefore provide something which it was not the role of Plowden to provide and that is a great unifying influence. This might prove to be its most permanent and perhaps most valuable contribution to progress and development within the educational system in Britain. Compartmentalism and isolationism within the British school system have been, and still are, absurdities which must now give way to a more rational and rewarding unity of purpose and to cooperation aimed at achieving a continuity in children's education which has been very largely absent.

During the last two decades the primary schools have lived through a period of ferment when new ideas, new methods and new approaches have been enthusiastically adopted, and new interpretations of their role developed. The vitality which Plowden saw and commended, lifted primary education on to a new plane. From this fertile period much has been gained which will endure to provide the base for future development, though not every new departure, different approach, new interpretation, has been completely successful or stood the tests of time and circumstance. Mistakes have been made, the pace has sometimes been too hot, consolidation has been lacking, ideas have not always been thoroughly understood before being put into practice, and new approaches and changes in classroom organization have been seized upon without sufficient evaluation as to their suitability for the situation into which they were to be introduced. As a result, some of what has taken place has been effective only superficially, lacking depth, and its value diminished because purposes and objectives were not clearly understood.

Allied to this eagerness to experiment with better and more interesting ways of encouraging children's learning was another factor which has contributed for good or ill to the condition of present primary education. This is the succession of waves of emphasis in different areas of the curriculum and organization in primary schools, which have rolled across the scene like surf across the ocean floor, carrying all before them. Although all worthy in themselves, and all stimulating interest and experiment in areas where these were needed, each surge attracted enthusiastic protagonists among the more lively, imaginative or ambitious. In the process other things were often left to one side and balance was lost. Each in turn became the mode of the moment and those teachers who were not bowled over by enthusiasm felt they should make the gesture or were hauled along unwillingly in the undertow.

Piaget, Cuisenaire, modern mathematics, the integrated day, primary science, for instance, took their turn in the centre of the stage, all valuable in themselves and rightly claiming a place in the sun, but the loser was the English language for which no new impetus emerged to seize the imagination and create an enthusiastic following in the primary school. This is not to say that English was totally neglected, rather it was relegated to a place of lesser importance while energy and enthusiasm were directed elsewhere. Time previously spent on language work was absorbed into other activities. Instead of language taking a foremost place in teaching across the curriculum, systematic and methodical language teaching was given less attention. Informal class organizations and the adoption of such approaches as the integrated day, project work, discovery and activity methods, integrated studies, should have provided for English to become the core of the curriculum. Instead, faculty understanding and organization of these approaches in the classroom often led to sterile and unrewarding use of language time and the opportunity was lost. The Bullock Report refers to a loss of coherence in the use of resources and in the organization of reading and writing activity. Its recommendations now provide an opportunity for reinstatement of language teaching to a central place in the curriculum.

The Bullock Report was born out of the rumblings of discontent which had been heard for some time about standards of education in the schools, particularly with regard to reading skills. These rumblings were mainly coupled with attacks on 'modern' and 'informal' methods and it was at the primary school that the finger was frequently pointed. There was little or no firm evidence and acceptable standards of comparison were missing, but the criticisms, although often extreme, generalized and uninformed, made an impression.

The feeling among teachers was defensive, but there was also concern. Primary-school teachers believed in their methods. They regarded the primary school as the dynamic source of forward movement in education. There had been for a long time, even before the Plowden Report, the confident assumption that the primary school had created the ideal learning environment. This view was widely held not only among teachers but by other people in the fields of education as well. The campaign against progressive methods and the criticisms of standards therefore came as a shock. Confidence began to ebb; uncertainty set in. Primary teachers once so sure about their methods began to worry about 'the basics'.

As one result of this, more attention was focused on reading; but often to the exclusion of other aspects of language teaching. At the same time, headteachers found that younger teachers had less knowledge and understanding of how to teach reading. The training colleges were blamed for having failed to give sufficient emphasis to reading in their courses. In fact, the period of change and innovation, the emergence of new methods and curriculum developments, and the uneven acceptance of these in schools had presented great difficulties to the colleges. There could be very considerable differences in the lifestyles of the primary schools in which their students would eventually teach. Because of the autonomy enjoyed by British schools in their choice of curriculum and organization, some had moved very little, some had gone to extremes and there were many variations between. Students had to be prepared for a wide range of possibilities. In their efforts to provide for this, some colleges produced a diversity of courses at the expense of time given to reading and language teaching.

The timing of the publication of the Report was, as it happens, opportune. It appeared at a time when public interest in what was happening in primary schools had been roused by the continuing criticism of standards, particularly of literacy. Its publication was shortly followed by the sensational publicity given by the media to the enquiry into the William Tyndale School[1] and by the publication of Neville Bennett's *Teaching Styles and Pupil Progress*[2] in January 1976, which was used selectively by the media, contrary to its author's intentions, to castigate the 'progressive', 'informal' schools. There was also the growing realization by teachers that they should perhaps look more closely at what they were doing so that criticism could be answered.

Ironically, the Plowden Report, for all the richness of its ideas, the acclaim with which it was received and the enthusiasm it engendered, has been blamed for some of the shortcomings seen by some in present standards. The argument is that excellent as the results of the Plowden approach are in the right hands, they call for able and experienced teaching to achieve these results and that there are too many teachers who are not able to plan successfully and monitor adequately. There is a degree of truth in this view, but it assumes what is by no means proven: a supposed comparative decline in standards from those supposed to have existed in the past.

Primary-school teachers do not accept the pessimistic talk about the decline in standards, but there is a genuine desire among them to face up to the climate which has been created by events and to examine their work. Since language is the core, they will turn to the Bullock Report for guidance. There is a feeling that there has been enough of change for the present and that a period of retrenchment, a redefinition of aims, clearer statements of objectives and a simplification of the curriculum are now needed. Not an abandonment of the gains of the past two decades nor a scramble 'back to basics', but rather more opportunity for study in depth by teachers of their objectives and organization, and by children in their learning activities.

For the first year of its life, though, the Bullock Report caused hardly a ripple at classroom level. Now, a surge of interest at all levels has arisen. This is the 'Year of the Bullock' as one Education Officer in Kent[3] has named it. Conferences, courses, meetings and discussion groups have begun to involve an increasing number of teachers who are recognizing the importance and the significance of the recommendations to be found in the Report. Many teachers are beginning to feel that Bullock represents a watershed in education – particularly education of the young. They are beginning to see in the Bullock Report the kind of positive statement they had seemed to lack and a timely reminder that the pendulum had perhaps swung too far.

What is particularly significant in the Report for the primary school? First and foremost it will bring the whole question of language teaching into focus. Schools will review their own situations against the observations and recommendations made. But it will not be left to schools alone; encouragement, even pressure, to look more closely at the provision for language teaching will come from education authorities, through their officers and inspectors, and from the Department of Education and Science through the inspectorate.

The emphasis given in the Report to closer contacts among schools is already bearing fruit. Teachers at all levels feel the need for more discussion among themselves. Traditional attitudes are softening, schools and teachers are beginning to find out more about one another and share problems. Although there are no doubt varying degrees of cooperation, generally schools in different and in the same age groups have existed as isolated units, exchanging nothing or little of their experiences, and not feeling the need to do so. Infant schools have had little or no communication with junior schools and secondary schools have ignored junior schools. True, written records of some kind usually pass on with the children as they move up from one school to the next, but coordination of methods, discussion of objectives, and the creation of understanding have been consistently lacking. There has indeed often been antipathy and suspicion between one school and another. There is also some evidence of this kind of attitude within schools where teachers have been inclined to isolate themselves in their classrooms and to resist efforts to coordinate the work of age groups or to concern themselves with the work of classes other than their own.

The insistence of Bullock on continuity between schools, whether in general terms or with language development specifically in view, is therefore likely to have important and lasting benefits for the junior school in its position as the link between infant and secondary stages.

The great emphasis the Report gives to the unity of the various modes of language use may mean that the fragmentation which has impoverished language teaching and led to neglect of some aspects of it in junior schools will be recognized. By giving support to the need for a sensible and relevant regard for spelling and handwriting, by insisting on the value of good standards of presentation, by questioning the real meaning of labels such as 'creative writing', 'free expression' etc. and by showing that all uses of language, productive as well as receptive contributed to intellectual development, Bullock brings into perspective the need for closer attention to English in all its diversity.

The Report draws attention to the lack of support suffered by English language teaching in terms of inspectorate, local education authority advisory services, and in schools through the failure to allocate scale posts for responsibility for the coordination of language teaching. If, as a result, the level of support is recognized as inadequate and action is taken, this could do a great deal to restore the pivotal position of language in the junior school, and indeed at all levels.

Bullock recognizes the need to provide training to reverse the lack of understanding about the operation of language and already there is movement towards this which will add momentum to the reviving interest in language which the Report has engendered. It has long been held that teachers of English lack a serviceable working description of the language. The suggestion that a body should be set up to find such a description, and perhaps find more exact definitions so that aims can be classified, must ultimately be beneficial in all spheres of language teaching.

Alleged deficiencies in reading led to the setting up of the

Bullock Committee but wisely the members saw their brief as a wider one and treated reading in the context of language as a whole. Nevertheless, Bullock has some very cogent things to say about reading and the teaching of reading. For instance, the suggestion that the idea of reading readiness has been misinterpreted will find support among some junior-school teachers who feel that this misinterpretation has been the cause of reading retardation in some children. Similarly, the attention given to phonics in the Report may convince some whose views are still coloured by earlier-held theories about the introduction of phonics, which often resulted in their being disregarded for too long. Concern with the unity of language activities as a means to literacy does not reduce the significance of reading but rather increases the need to look more closely at what is being done about it in junior schools, and at how the teaching of reading is being related to their language work.

There has always been concern for reading standards among teachers of junior children, and probably nothing engenders so much worry as the feeling that reading standards are poor. Probably more time and concentration of effort have been given to achieving reading competence and overcoming reading retardation than have been given to any other aspect of learning at this stage, but perhaps much of this effort has been misdirected and only partially successful. It has almost certainly been directed more at achieving word recognition and a reading vocabulary than at meaning. This emphasis also has tended to isolate reading from other aspects of language.[4]

Other shortcomings are evident. Many primary-school teachers lack knowledge and understanding of how children learn to read and the techniques of teaching reading. Teachers of older primary-school children have felt that reading competence should have been achieved earlier and are dismayed at the prospect of having to teach the earlier stages of reading themselves. There has been a tendency to look for solutions to reading problems in the withdrawal of children from the classroom into remedial groups outside it, and a reluctance, arising from feelings of inadequacy, to deal energetically and methodically with the reading organization within the classroom for slower and less competent readers. Too much is taken for granted once children have learned the basic skills; and where skills have been learned there is a failure to develop them.

In the junior school there has been recognition and understanding of how children learn in the whole context of their intellectual development. Active learning methods have flourished, particularly where reading is concerned; but there has been too much preoccupation with teaching and too little with learning.[5] What the Bullock Report has to say about reading and teaching reading is positive, down-to-earth and practical. It points to shortcomings and misconceptions and its message is too urgent to be ignored or forgotten. The signs are that it will not be, and that teachers in junior schools, indeed all teachers of whatever age group, will be reassessing their role and their capability in the matter of teaching reading. Those who train teachers, those who initiate courses, and those who have influence as advisers and inspectors, as well as teachers themselves, are already increasing their involvement in the move forward which the Bullock Report has accelerated. In the light of the Report, heads and teachers in junior schools will be reexamining their provision for teaching reading, which indeed in many schools is already excellent. In doing this they will look towards helping children to learn and to acquire the associated language skills while making sure that the way they teach is related to the way children learn.

The suggestion in the Report which gives respectability to specialism related to the junior school will provoke discussion. Junior-school teachers tend to regard specialism as stifling and essentially a secondary-school matter. The strong opposition in junior schools to the middle-school concept was largely due to the assumption that secondary-school influence based on specialization, formal attitudes, and methods dictated by the examination system, would seep downwards into lower age groups, and that younger children would be absorbed into the specialized subject-teaching pattern regarded as contrary to primary-school ideas of what is appropriate for children's learning at that stage.

Although Bullock does not envisage English as a specialist subject for younger children, it does recommend the presence of specialist help in junior schools. This will be seen as encouragement for the appointment of teachers with special qualifications and responsibility for language teaching in a school and its coordination across the curriculum. Their role would be to give support to their colleagues in planning and carrying out their work in English. There would be no difficulty in appointments being made within the provision for scale posts and undoubtedly this will happen. The initial difficulty might be in finding teachers well qualified to fill them.

Assertions of declining reading standards and reactions to these always come up against the same obstacle – the complete lack of reliable and acceptable standards of measurement and comparison. The Bullock Report states the importance of historical perspective and the need for realistic means of assessment and proposes a national monitoring procedure. In response to this, a unit concerned with assessment and performance has been set up, since the publication of the Report, within the Department of Education and Science. Its task is to look into existing methods of assessing children, to improve them, to promote assessment and to identify significant differences of achievement.

While agreeing on the need for more comprehensive and reliable assessment procedures and recognizing their potential value, teachers will also be concerned about their nature and function and the way in which they are applied. There is some apprehension that the testing procedures might create pressure on the infant schools from junior schools to push children along the path of reading in such a way that their enjoyment of reading is overlooked. Teachers in both infant and junior schools fear there could be overuse of standardized tests, and it would be up to education authorities and teachers to agree on an appropriate selection and use of such tests as may become available, so that they would provide the greatest impetus to the purpose for which they are advocated – the raising of standards of literacy in the broadest sense.

There are few concerned with education in Great Britain who would quarrel with the assertion that the teaching of English at all levels is in need of reform, but it would be wrong to take too pessimistic a view of the state of affairs which gives rise to this motion. In spite of the clamour of criticism, education in British primary schools is alive and well. There is movement and enthusiasm and much that is sound and worthy of imitation. The natural process of assimilation and change is itself regulating some of the practices which have failed the test of time and might have contributed to some of the shortcomings to which Bullock draws attention.

The Bullock Report, like other reports, was in some respects out of date when it was published and much that it recommends is already common practice in schools, but no junior school should ignore or fail to profit by its immense value as a source book for successful language teaching. As the conclusion to its appraisal of the Report, The National Association of Head-teachers (1975) says this:

The Bullock Report, by pinpointing deficiences, offering suggestions for improvement and outlining recommendations covering all the services involved in education, has provided many starting points for consultation at all levels and for all agencies. Talking can be started immediately. It does not involve resources; it is not expensive in terms of money; it merely involves or demands time.

And, it might be added, resolution and goodwill.

REFERENCE

NAHT (1975) *A Language for Life (An Appraisal by the National Association of Headteachers)* Haywards Heath, England: National Association of Headteachers

NOTES

1   The headmaster and some members of staff of the William Tyndale Primary School in London were accused by other members of staff, by some parents and by some School Managers, of causing breakdowns in standards of learning achievement and discipline through the use of extreme progressive teaching methods. At a subsequent Official Enquiry there was criticism of all the factions involved, including the headmaster, the education authority and the inspectorate.

2   In *Teaching Styles and Pupil Progress* (Open Books 1976), Neville Bennett reports his investigations which set out to answer two basic questions: 'Do differing teaching styles result in disparate pupil progress?' and 'Do different types of pupil perform better under certain styles of teaching?' His conclusions appear to indicate that formal teaching methods were generally more effective than informal methods.

3 John Fogarty, MA, Divisional Education Officer, Tunbridge Wells, Kent.
4 See Margaret Spencer in H. Rosen (1975) (Ed.) *Language and Literacy in our Schools: Some Appraisals of the Bullock Report* University of London Institute of Education.
5 Again see Margaret Spencer's article.

A blaze of obscurity: 'Bullock' in the comprehensive school

Ramin Minovi

This article is based on the impressions I have received as a teacher of English (Head, or Chairman, of Department) in a comprehensive school in the West Midlands of England; and in conversations and discussions with other teachers and education-ists, often at conferences and meetings organized by the National Association for the Teaching of English, and occasionally by other agencies. It should be understood that the views expressed are my own, and like any other views not actually backed up by specific research, they are necessarily informed by my own pre-judices and experiences. It seems to me that this is as it should be: until research is commissioned on the extent to which the recommendations of Bullock are being implemented in schools, impressions are all we have to go on; and in any case they have always played an important part in fleshing out the body of which statistics can be no more than the skeleton.

To understand the reception of a report like Bullock, we need some grasp of the attitude of the average (or even above-average) teacher in England towards published research on education. I think it is only a slight overstatement to say that this attitude is, and has always been, one of profound distrust; and it manifests itself in an unwillingness to read, think about, discuss, or acknow-ledge the existence of anything that might generally be con-sidered under the heading of research, and which might have something new to say about the content and method of the teacher's discipline. It's not unusual to find secondary-school teachers using notes which they made while still undergraduates as almost the only basis of their teaching, even ten years after they began work; and many lean fairly heavily on the commercial textbooks in use in their particular schools, which may be even more out of date. In my own school I found teachers using, in

1971, and even with remedial classes, copies of a textbook which had been produced specifically for use in selective grammar schools in 1946.

Together with this distrust towards research goes a belief that the personal education of the teacher reaches a sort of maximum saturation level at the moment he completes his initial training and begins teaching. He has little or nothing further to learn about his subject, and he now enters on a separate phase of his career in which he applies or passes on what he has learned. We may regard this as 'practice', using the word much as we do in medicine, but the teacher is more likely to think of it, and to refer to it as 'experience'. From now on, this 'experience' will be the most highly-valued commodity he can acquire and offer again in the teaching market; and he will become progressively warier towards those who, having left the classroom, presume to reenter the educational arena by writing books, taking part in working parties which compile reports, do research, and so on. The metaphor of the mine is often used to emphasize the distinction between those who work at the face, and those whose lives are passed on the surface, in the sun and air, and who can have no real conception of the difficulties and hardships faced by the men who actually hew the coal.

I have said that I am only slightly overstating the case. I'm sure that it is no overstatement at all to say that only a minority of teachers (less than 50 per cent) are ever more up-to-date than they were at the moment when they completed their initial training. The only evidence I could offer to support this view would be anecdotal: in a school employing at least 150 staff over a period of six years (about seventy at any one time), only five attended courses of any kind during those six years; and four of those undoubtedly did so primarily to enhance their promotion prospects, rather than to add to their knowledge or skills. Of seventy staff in another school (thirty-five of them university graduates rather than college of education trained, and therefore considered by themselves and by their employers as superior teachers), only *one* had heard of (and read) as well-known a book as Bloom's *Taxonomy of Cognitive Objectives*. In an English Department of seven staff, two had heard of, and one had read, Dixon's *Growth through English*, nine years after its publication. Experienced teachers who start Open University courses, or take a year's sabbatical (usually seconded on full pay) to read for a degree, are often bewildered when they confront the sheer quantity of published material that exists, so firmly is it taken for granted that teachers have neither the time nor the inclination to keep abreast of advances and developments in their own subjects.

On the other hand, it is only fair to point out that the demands upon the classroom teacher are now very great and increasing all the time. In addition to preparing and teaching around thirty-five forty-minute lessons each week (most schools work a forty-period week), he will have numerous other duties, which it would be tedious to list in detail, but all of which take their toll in time and energy. An interesting byproduct of the recent publicity (much of it greatly exaggerated and sensationalized) given to the 'blackboard jungle' side of modern secondary-school life is a quite novel and fairly widespread sympathy for the plight of the teacher among members of the public. An attitude of 'I wouldn't have your job at any price' has, to some extent, replaced envy of teachers' long holidays. The educational cuts of the last three years mean that classes are larger, and resources fewer, than they have been for some years, and it may be that we shall look back on the mid-1960s and early 1970s as a golden age – a prospect that seemed pretty unlikely at the time, but that's the way with golden ages. The Educational Publishers Council recently published figures which suggest that, set against the general retail price index, expenditure on books reached a peak of £6.50 per schoolchild in 1973, but by 1976 this figure had fallen to under £5.00. If this rate of decrease were to be maintained, the figure would reach zero just in time for 1984.

I referred above to the proliferation of unfavourable publicity in the press. This has often revolved around the idea that the reason standards are falling (this is always taken for granted) is that bunches of airy-fairy educationists are constantly descending from cloud-cuckooland and foisting upon teachers and their charges a mass of untried fiddle-faddle which is then damned indiscriminately as 'progressive' methods. In fact, controversy in the press about changing or so-called progressive methods usually bears little relationship to the situation in schools; the controversial methods can, in the first place, be seen in use in only a small number of schools; and what is more, they are often misapplied and misunderstood by both teachers and educational journalists. Teachers are no better at describing, for the benefit of laymen, what they are trying to do and why they are trying to do it, than are electricians or professional football players.

The last point I want to make is related to both this, to the distrust of research, and to the value of experience. It is that the wisdom of the profession is embodied in what can only be described as a collection of rules of thumb which form the most powerful weapon in the teacher's armoury and are often encapsulated in apocryphal tales and a kind of folk myth. It is not entirely in jest that a prominent trade unionist has called the National Union of Teachers 'the last surviving medieval craft guild'. Thus the true ability of the successful teacher is something that cannot be quantified or even identified because it remains in the unmapped terrain of human capacities. This belief has important implications for one of Bullock's principal findings: that no matter what methods are used, the teacher is the most important factor in academic success in schools.

Here I would like to remind the reader that most of my examples and illustrations are drawn from schools in Birmingham and the West Midlands where I teach. It might be unfair to suppose that they applied to schools and teachers throughout the country; but my conversations with teachers from elsewhere, and my visits to other schools, lead me to think that my impressions are largely representative.

This was the context in which the Bullock Report appeared in February 1975. Commentators were quick to point out that the Report eschews 'easy' solutions and simplified remedies for the alleged fall in standards. Most surprising, in the eyes of the press, was the Report's failure to admit that standards were indeed falling. In addition, its unexpected bulk was daunting, and nobody seemed to know quite what to say. One of the immediate results was that such publicity as the Report received in the first few days concentrated to a great extent on Stuart Froome's minority report. Mr Froome was a primary-school headmaster, and his report is based on misconceptions about the nature and functions of language that have bedevilled mother-tongue teaching in England for generations. In a rather quaint nineteenth-century way he regards the *written* not only as the highest, but, apparently, as the primary form of the language:

> I believe the Committee is in error in putting undue emphasis upon talking as a means of learning language. It has its place, but in my view, one of the causes of the decline in English standards today is the recent drift in schools away from the written to the spoken word. (p. 559)

Mr Froome is convinced that standards of literacy have indeed fallen, and he reiterates the old belief that teaching children grammar enables them to write better:

> It could also have been stated with greater force that the more competent children are in the trained accomplishments of spelling, punctuation and the grammatical arrangement of words, the more likely are they to write vividly, gracefully and tellingly . . . (p. 556)

Mr Froome offers no evidence to support this view, and such as we have from other sources suggests that it is utterly unfounded. Nevertheless, few would deny that people learn to improve their written competence through practice. He defends reading tests, described as inadequate in the body of the Report, by saying 'they are the only ones we have' – which is not the strongest position in the world.

The appeal of his 'Note of dissent', which takes up only four pages, lies in its shortness and simplicity. It is the kind of statement people expect from headmasters: stern, minatory, a bit pompous; but at the same time reassuring, and implying that there are indeed simple remedies for what we all know is a bad state of affairs if we're only prepared to admit it. Really, it's just a matter of hard work and the acquisition of a bit of knowledge. He sees 'correctness' in language as something about which there can be little argument, and regards grammar as a set of prescriptive rules which we break at our peril. It is a view undoubtedly held by a majority of teachers and in fact by most people. It accords with the view of the best-selling English textbook writer Ronald Ridout, who usually contrives to condemn what he identifies as the 'creative English school' whenever he is interviewed. He is quick to jump aboard any bandwagon, however, and his workbook for adult illiterates, published shortly after Bullock (which, of course, contains a chapter on the problem) had sold several hundred thousand within the year.

Teachers were in much the same position as the press. The handful who had heard of the Committee knew, or thought they knew, that the Report was about reading standards, and they weren't prepared for such an exhaustive document. For once, therefore, it was local authority advisers and inspectors who did most to set in motion the implementation of those parts of the Report that captured their imaginations. By whatever agency, the Report's existence and even a few garbled accounts of what it said about some matters of concern gradually filtered through to the secondary schools; but to use words like 'impact' in connection with its arrival would be to indulge in hyperbole. Michael Marland's comment that the 'gut reaction throughout the country was that the Report carried sound practical sense' is too sanguine. Whose gut? Certainly not that of the average secondary-school classroom teacher.

But Marland is certainly right on two other counts: first, that the Report was at the same time so massive, yet so lacking in specific detail, that schools took from it what they wanted; and second, that the focus for secondary schools in particular was the Report's call for a school policy on *language across the curriculum*. Since it is dealt with elsewhere, I will confine myself to one or two comments about how and why this interest was aroused, and what it led to in schools.

Firstly, although the idea was new to the great majority of teachers, a good deal of work had been done in the field, largely under the auspices of the London Association for the Teaching of English and the National Association for the Teaching of English. *Language, the Learner, and the School* had been published in 1969 (Barnes), and it contained a short discussion document prepared by Harold Rosen with the title 'Towards a language policy across the curriculum'. The concept had been presented to groups of teachers at conferences and courses, and following its Annual Conference in 1971, a whole issue of NATE's journal *English in Education* had been devoted to it. By

1975 the School Council's Project *Writing Across the Curriculum* was in its final phase; and although the book was not to be published until April 1976 (Martin *et al.*), the Project prepared 'packs' of what amounted to evidence submitted by teachers, and pamphlets about writing in secondary schools. It is, I suppose, natural that members of organizations like NATE often make the mistake of assuming that their esoteric knowledge is general; and I think it is true to say that little was known about language across the curriculum beyond a fairly small circle. Bullock changed that: six months later the phrase might be heard in any one of Birmingham's 125 secondary schools.

Secondly, the idea aroused interest among local education authority advisers and education officers, and many sent out memos to their headmasters which asked, in effect: 'What are you doing about a language policy in your school?' The Inner London Education Authority made such a demand of all its schools, and so did Birmingham LEA. Primary-school heads were able to reply that the question didn't really apply to them because in few of their schools was the curriculum explicit divided into many subjects with barriers of varying rigidity between them; but a rash of language across the curriculum projects sprang up in secondary schools.

As the Report had suggested, these projects were usually initiated by the headmaster in response to the education authority's request, and a senior member of staff put in charge. It was assumed that he would work closely with the head of the English Department. A number of methods were employed to get the projects moving. Some worked reasonably well, and a working party would be set up and busy itself in various activities, like following one particular pupil around for a week and recording all the different kinds of writing he was asked to do. A few were such disastrous failures that they resulted in internecine feuds and a good deal of bitterness in some staff commonrooms.

The idea was, inevitably, widely misunderstood. A science teacher expressed the feeling of many teachers when he said to me, 'We might as well give this method a try; they're not learning anything by the present methods we're using.' I would suggest that it is because of this misunderstanding that language across the curriculum became accepted with so little fuss: most teachers thought it was a new *teaching* method, and, ever optimistic, hoped that this time it might really be the instant answer to all their problems. My own branch of the NATE maintained a working party and held an open meeting on language across the curriculum which was attended by a large number of teachers from subject areas other than English. A deputy headmaster, a geographer by training, who had been asked to attend by his headmaster, felt that his time had been wasted when he found that he had not been provided with a set of blueprints or lesson plans; this, he said, was not what he had come to hear. He didn't want to face the implications that lie behind the phrase 'The pupils' engagement with the subject may rely upon a linguistic process that (the teacher's) procedures actually discourage'. The schools where successful projects were initiated were the ones that avoided direct approaches; yet it remains to be seen whether many secondary-school headmasters, having put themselves in a position where they can say to their education officers, 'Yes, I am doing something about it', will allow much more time or effort to be spent on further work, or will actually push ahead to the stage where they can say, 'Yes, we have a *policy*: this is what it consists of'. My own experience suggests that in many schools the projects have been seen as purges on slackness in such matters as handwriting and spelling. Requests for whole-day conferences for the entire staff of a school have been generally turned down, but they have taken place in some schools.

Those working on 'language' projects or study groups in schools will have picked up a good deal of knowhow about how teachers see themselves. I have already remarked that they are not good at describing what they are doing. Many, particularly the more experienced, have described their work as dull or ordinary, when in the eyes of the enquirers it seemed to be a model of good practice; others make large claims for themselves when all the evidence suggests that their progressivism is merely surface decoration, and they are, in fact, either as conventional as one could wish, or in control of chaos.

Altogether, this section (Chapter 12), has received attention disproportionate to the space (six pages) devoted to it in the Report; yet despite this attention, it seems to me that the fundamental importance of the concepts subsumed in the phrase 'language across the curriculum' will be grasped only very slowly in secondary education. The teaching methods of some individuals may be affected, however, so there remains a chance that headway will be made.

Another phrase that captured the imagination of headmasters, especially those who were not themselves English specialists, was 'instrument of policy'. Notes went out to heads of English Departments on the following lines:

> The matter of the English syllabus about which I spoke to you is best explained in the following extract from the Bullock Report. I should be glad if in dealing with the major questions of English teaching such as oral language, reading, writing and literature, consideration could also be given to drama, books and school library, teaching aids, needs of immigrant children, testing and examining the records.

The extract referred to was from Chapter 15, paragraph 30:

> Every English Department should produce a document making clear its purposes and the means it proposes to fulfil them. . . . We believe that the thinking that emerges . . . should take shape in a manifesto, reflecting the spirit and purpose of the department and responsive to the continuing exchange of views with it. We suggest that the term 'instrument of policy' would represent this more accurately than 'syllabus' or 'scheme of work'.

There is no doubt that some departments did a good deal of thinking, and rethinking, and produced such 'instruments'. Others kept their headmasters quiet with old-fashioned syllabuses bearing fancy names. Whatever the true nature of the document, it's likely that the kinds of beliefs and attitudes I outlined in my introductory paragraphs would result in its being either used slavishly as a kind of course book, or totally ignored. I remember being begged for a copy of my department's syllabus by a young nonspecialist teacher who had been assigned to us to take one class during a staff shortage. Without opening it, she laid it on a table where it remained for a fortnight until it was buried under papers, when I took it away again. I mention this merely because I think it exemplifies the attitude of many teachers to the syllabus.

The third point which attracted notice was the revelation that as many as 32.8 per cent of all those teachers engaged in teaching English in secondary schools were considered by the Committee to have no discernible qualifications for doing so. It was only a revelation because no one had ever sat down and counted before, but once it had been made, the response was a dismissive shrug. What else could you expect? It has always been assumed that being a native speaker of English is sufficient qualification to teach it, and the slogan 'Every teacher is a teacher of English' has been misapplied (that is, 'therefore anyone can do it') to justify the inadequate staffing of English Departments.

In February 1976, a year after publication, the *Times Educational Supplement* held a 'Bullock Plus One' seminar in London to which they invited fifty teachers and educationists. The mood, while not actually euphoric, was optimistic, and caution was out of place. It was an occasion for large public statements which would look well in the paper's next two or three editions, and plain tales from the classroom were not called for.

In order to get some idea of the Report's reception in secondary schools, I presented a simple questionnaire to 250 teachers in five Birmingham comprehensive schools. The 250 were divided by subjects as follows:

English	30	Remedial	16
Mathematics	30	Home economics	14
Modern languages	21	Art and craft	23
Sciences	32	Physical education	9
History and allied subjects	48	Secretarial	4
Geography	17	Music	6

By experience, they were grouped as follows:

1–5 years	105
5–10 years	82
10–20 years	36
20–30 years	31
30 + years	4

This is fairly representative for an education authority which lost a large number of experienced staff between 1972 and 1974, and had to replace them with young teachers. The 31 in the 20–30 years' experience group consists entirely of headmasters (4), deputy heads and other administrative staff (21), and some heads of departments (6).

These were the questions and answers:

1   What subject do you teach?
2   How long have you been teaching?
3   Have you heard of the Bullock Report?   Yes 246   No 4
4   Have you read the Report?   Yes   9   No 241
5   Have you read a summary or outline?   Yes 160   No 90
6   The subject of the Bullock Report is
    (a) The teaching of science in primary schools   0
    (b) The reduction of school staffing in relation to a
        falling population   0
    (c) Reading and the use of English   84
    (d) A survey of the fall in reading standards   81
    (e) Language across the curriculum   81
    (f) Don't know   4
7   The title of the Bullock Report is
    (a) Language across the Curriculum   69
    (b) Reading: A Matter for Concern   106
    (c) Learning the Language of Science   0
    (d) A Language for Life   67
    (e) Schools of the Future: The Language of Economics   0
    (f) Don't know   8
8   Is the Report, in your opinion,
    Good 52   Poor 6   Neither 88   Don't know 104

It is hardly a detailed or profound piece of research, and the figures are not in any way sensational or even surprising, but some further points emerged when I talked to some of the teachers who completed the questionnaire. I had at least brief conversation with well over half the sample, and I made a point of questioning further all those who claimed to have read the Report, when it became clear that none of them had in fact done so. They had followed the perfectly reasonable procedure of reading the bits they thought would apply to their own situations, and the 'best performance' was by a headmaster who had read eleven of the twenty-six chapters. One of those who claimed to have read the whole Report had in fact read only two chapters amounting to twenty-one pages. A whole science department (seven teachers) in one of the schools had sat round with a copy of the Report making sure that all their answers were correct, although I had requested that the questionnaire be completed from memory. Another school had no copy of its own, and had been obliged to borrow a copy from the local library on an earlier occasion. The fact that they had earlier admitted to not having read either the Report or a summary did not prevent two people from condemning it as poor and three from describing it as good, but this might have been just carelessness. I think that the multiple-choice form adopted for speed and ease in questions 6 and 7 gave considerable help and much more ignorance would have been revealed if the questions had been 'What is the subject?' and 'What is the title?'

Still, people were generally aware that a Report had been published, and most of them believed that it had something to do with the teaching of English or reading.

Many of Bullock's recommendations imply the spending of money, and large sums of money, on both teachers and other resources. It has been recognized for some time that English departments, in common with other humanities areas, have been poorly provided with resources, specialist rooms, staff and ancillary help, in comparison with, say, science departments. Bullock speaks of soundproofed projection theatres and recording studios, English department suites, space for informal work, greatly improved storage and retrieval of resources of all kinds, a minimum of twenty hours' assistance per week per five forms of entry from ancillary helpers, and lightweight stacking furniture. I have no doubt at all that I speak for the great majority of heads of English departments when I say that my own department possesses literally none of these advantages. Only one of the rooms used for English teaching has storage space, and, at a pinch, any room is considered good enough to teach English in.

The Committee comment (15: 26):

We do not underestimate the financial problems of equipping English departments in the ways we have suggested. A realistic view makes it obvious that sweeping changes and improvements cannot be effected overnight. Nevertheless, we do believe that where building improvements are being planned or new projects designed opportunities such as those we have described should not be missed. (p. 235)

Unfortunately, since February 1975, economic considerations have effectively destroyed any hope of expansion of any kind in the education services of this country for at least a decade. A falling birthrate, allied to the popular belief that thirty and forty are ideal numbers respectively for secondary and primary classes, is about to bring about the closure of more than thirty colleges of education. A large number of newly qualified teachers have been unable to find work because education authorities are reducing their staffing establishments. Far from being improved, staffing ratios are being worsened, and class sizes increasing. Primary schools in my own city have been ordered to shut off classrooms not constantly in use in order to save heat and light. The recommended expansion of the advisory service will not take place. My own allowance for buying books was reduced by 15 percent in 1975 and by over 30 percent in 1976. That is, the amount I had been told I could spend was reduced by over 40 percent ten weeks after the start of the financial year, and a little was returned ten months later. It would be depressing to list the ways in which education will suffer over the next five to ten years; suffice to say that sheer economic considerations will wipe out many of Bullock's recommendations and reduce drastically much of the influence it might have had. As Dr Halsey remarked at the Bullock Plus One Seminar, 'It is possible to *buy* changes of attitude.'

I see one other major hindrance to the acceptance of Bullock's views and recommendations. I refer to the general belief, now apparently stronger than ever, that no matter what Bullock said, standards are falling and it's time we did something about it. A more cautious view, which I have heard expressed by a number of liberal educationists, is that while standards may not actually be falling, they are not, and have never been, good enough. The

Prime Minister's call, in a 1976 speech, for 'a curriculum for crisis', and the setting up of regional conferences by the Secretary of State for Education, Mrs Shirley Williams, have been referred to as manifestations of 'the Bullock backlash'. I do not think this is a fair or accurate description. More significant factors are the Black Papers published by a group of diehard descendants of Thomas Gradgrind, and the findings of a research project led by Neville Bennett, published in April 1976 as *Teaching Styles and Pupil Progress*.

This purported to show that 'formal' methods of teaching produce better results than 'informal' methods. Neither term was clearly defined, and the fact that nearly all existing tests and examinations are designed to measure that which can be formally taught and easily quantified was ignored. Nevertheless, like the textbooks of Mr Ridout, and Mr Froome's 'Note of Dissent', it is what people want to hear. Even teachers were reassured by learning that *informal* methods demand more skill, time and energy. What greater incentive could be offered for clinging (I will not speak of returning) to comparatively mechanistic instruction? There has been, as Hamlet would have learned from Guildenstern, 'much throwing about of brains'. There has been a good deal of question-begging, too. The Prime Minister wished to align himself and his Government behind 'a commitment not merely to raise standards in schools, but to ensure also that they teach what society needs'.

What, then, have been the effects of the Bullock Report in secondary schools? Some are tangible, others are difficult to identify. Headmasters and many other teachers have been at least reminded that language is the means by which we learn, and some have learned it for the first time. Some remedial departments have received extra money, help, advice and even staff. Many English departments have been made to write down their aims and objectives, if not actually to think about and discuss them. By and large, I am forced to conclude that the effect of Bullock has so far been negligible; but that so substantial a document should disappear without trace is not to be believed. Bullock *is* an important book, it *is* full of practical and sound commonsense; but it is not precisely a manifesto, nor is it a set of normative rules. It indicates directions and identifies concerns;

but they have been for a long time, and will continue to be for longer yet, the concerns of a minority of teachers. John Watts, in his Chairman's address to NATE's 1975 Conference, said: 'Bullock in effect says to NATE – Your concerns have been the right ones, but teachers of English in the classrooms know nothing of you'. With the omission of the word 'English', much the same could be said of the Bullock Report. That is not a pessimistic statement: it is a warning that the fight is not yet won, but it carries with it the suggestion that it *can* be won. In twenty-five years' time I expect that Bullock will be seen as only one of the important milestones in the progress towards real education in our schools.

REFERENCES

BARNES, D. (1969) *Language, the Learner and the School* Harmondsworth, England: Penguin

BENNETT, N. (1976) *Teaching Styles and Pupil Progress* London: Open Books

MARTIN, N., D'ARCY, P., NEWTON, B. and PARKER, R. (1976) *Writing and Learning Across the Curriculum 11–16* London: Ward Lock Educational

6 Research implications of the Report

INTRODUCTION

As Charles Cooper points out in the opening article of this section, the Bullock Report is rich in implications for research on language and literacy teaching in schools. Some of these implications are stated rather directly in the Report; others need to be drawn out from various recommendations made in it.

Cooper helpfully lists what he sees as the key research hypotheses on literary study and writing contained in the Report. He discusses these hypotheses in the light of current research methods and findings in these two areas, making suggestions when he can about how future research might be conducted which would be sound and would be 'likely to have direct impact on classroom teaching'.

Don Graves praises the Committee's report for the 'stance' it takes on literacy issues and the general sense of direction it provides for learning and teaching. At the same time, he criticizes the Committee for its failure to provide the kind of 'specifics' which will help classroom teachers, especially in the teaching of writing. He then draws on his own observational and case-study research on the writing processes of seven year olds to provide clearer and more concrete guidance for teachers in helping younger children develop their writing abilities.

Despite the concreteness of his findings and recommendations, Graves admits that 'the map for the writing process and the developmental profiles of young children has been barely sketched in'. We need more careful descriptive research on the writing processes of pupils of all ages, and these studies must take into account a wide range of variables.

Echoing Cooper and Graves, Robert Parker argues strongly that teachers should have a role in designing and conducting this needed 'action-research', and that it should arise directly from practical questions about their own individual and collective efforts in teaching for literacy. If, over time, these 'action-research' projects become more systematic, more rigorous, more tied to theory, and more significant in the results they produce, then their impact will spread beyond individual schools or school systems to affect both theory and practice nationally and, perhaps, internationally as well.

Surveying English teaching practices and assessing national performance

Charles R. Cooper

INTRODUCTION
As other articles in this collection make clear *A Language for Life* offers rich suggestions for English programmes and for classroom instruction. I can report that it is also rich in implications for research on teaching literature and writing. In addition, it contains a survey instrument of great interest to researchers and a proposal for a system of national monitoring or assessment which will attract the attention of state and national assessors in America.

I will report on the survey and the monitoring system and draw out from the Report the research implications for literary study and writing. Because of space limitations I must exclude consideration of general reading, although this is a major concern in the Report, where there are clearly a number of research implications, particularly for measurement issues like screening and diagnosis. I have limited myself to the reading of literature because this kind of reading remains the primary concern of secondary English teachers in America. In discussing the research implications for literary study and writing, I have in mind older students in secondary-school classrooms, and I am addressing an audience of British and American English education research specialists and classroom teachers prepared to carry out research studies.

One of the most attractive features of the Report is the insistence that classroom teachers must begin doing research in their own schools:

We see as the first priority to need the give teachers greater insight into educational research, a process which should begin during initial training and find expression in inservice education. Wherever possible this should involve them in the research work itself, from collecting survey data to formulating and testing hypotheses and evaluating results.

The writers of the Report chose 'to lay emphasis on the need for research and teaching to become more closely interrelated' rather than to draw up lists of research questions or projects. They also pointedly encourage an increase in the kind of research that is likely to have direct impact on classroom teaching. In that spirit, I emphasize research questions close to the concerns of teachers, questions teachers could attempt to answer in their own schools. It is interesting to note that the insistence in the Report that teachers become involved in research comes at a time when English education and reading research in America are beginning to encompass less technical research models like case studies and participant observation. These are just the models which teachers can most easily use in their own classrooms.

RESEARCHING LITERARY STUDY

Teachers and researchers interested in research on response to literature, teaching literature, and reading interests should know *Literature and the Reader* by Alan Purves and Richard A. Beach (1972). A more recent review (Cooper 1976) seeks to update the Purves and Beach review of studies in the area of response to literature, and a recent annotated bibliography (Monson and Peltola 1976), lists a variety of kinds of studies in children's literature.

In the Report itself most of the research questions have to do with the *teaching* of literature. They direct us towards discovering the ideal conditions under which literature might be presented to class groups. The main concern of the Report is with the possibilities of voluntary or individualized reading. The general instructional approach recommended by the Report seems to be guided free reading or sustained silent reading, complemented by careful class study of an occasional text, preferably a modern one. Poetry is not neglected. The teacher's role would be one of explorer of the text with the students and of conscientious, supportive monitor of their free reading. This general instructional approach already has what little research support is available for classroom literary study. But even though at present we have clear support for the main features of the instructional approach recommended in the Report, we need newer studies in different contexts to confirm the findings of older studies.

Let me list here briefly what seems to me to be the key research hypotheses from the chapter on literary study in the Report:

1 *An increase in the amount and range of guided free reading of literature will improve students' ability to read literature and will contribute to general language development and to basic literacy.* In an important summary statement the Report has this to say about literary study:

> We have emphasized that learning to read is a developmental process which continues over the years. To read intelligently is to read responsively; it is to ask questions of the text and use one's own framework of experience in interpreting it. In working his way through a book the reader imparts, projects, anticipates, speculates on alternative outcomes; and nowhere is this process more active than in imaginative literature. We strongly recommend that there should be a major effort to increase voluntary reading, which should be recognized as a powerful instrument for the improvement of standards.

Indirect evidence to support this recommendation comes from the psycholinguistic or information-processing view of the fluent reading process (Smith 1971; Cooper and Petrosky 1976), where the most important contribution to reading development is seen simply as large amounts of reading practice in real books, not in 'readers' or in workbooks. More direct evidence for the recommendation comes from findings of curriculum evaluation studies comparing extensive to intensive literary study. The Purves and Beach review summarizes this research as follows:

> One curriculum practice has been well studied, and the results of each study tend to confirm the others. The practice is that of comparing 'the rapid reading of a comparatively large number of literary works with general comments and discussions in

class' (the extensive method) with 'the detailed analytic study of the minimum of literary work' (the intensive method) . . . the only sure evidence we have of the efficacy of any variable is that related to extensive reading. The studies generally confirm that extensive reading is as effective as intensive reading in certain ways, particularly as regards critical reading achievement and attitude.

These studies need to be confirmed in different settings for different age levels. We now have better measure and better curriculum-evaluation designs than those used in most of the early studies of extensive reading.

2   *Growth in 'discernment' or 'appreciation' comes about only with the close study of certain carefully-selected texts.* I have stated this hypothesis in the 'null' form and placed it here to raise an important question about the first hypothesis above. That question might be stated as follows: even though it may be true that students can learn to read literature with more insight – to comprehend it better – merely through guided free reading, does it necessarily follow that their taste will improve, that they will come to prefer literature of higher quality? The Report itself seems ambivalent on this point. Even though the measurement problems are complex (Cooper 1972), this hypothesis can be directly tested in a curriculum-evaluation study.

3   *Teacher influence and book provision are the critical factors in improving reading ability in the secondary years.* Teachers need to learn what is available, to read widely themselves, particularly in fiction written especially for adolescents; and schools need to have more systematic procedures for book acquisition. The Report says, 'The building up of book resources is often something of a piecemeal process rather than a planned response to defined objectives.' Certainly an emphasis on free reading in the literature programme would require more book resources than are presently available in many schools. While we can be guided in book ordering by the vast amount of research on reading interest, we really know very little about the factors of teacher influence. What is it that effective teachers do? How do they get

their students to read so much? What might we learn from observing effective teachers in action?

4 *In order to expand the range of free reading during the secondary years, teachers and schools must keep a record of the books students read.* This hypothesis would lead us to test the importance of the teacher's *monitoring* function in free reading. Over the six years between grades seven and twelve a student would read dozens of books. A record of all these books with brief annotations for each would reveal a pattern of choice and would enable teachers to make available to a student kinds of books outside his or her range of choices. For example, a student who has not read a short-story collection or a biography might be encouraged to do so.

5 *Fictional literature is a useful adjunct to the study of informational topics in other subjects.* We need to know a great deal more about the relation of fiction to the study of history, psychology or the sciences.

6 *The most favourable condition for class study of the same text is 'when teacher and taught approach it in a common spirit of exploration'.* This hypothesis calls for us to test the effectiveness of the teacher as 'naive reader' rather than as expert dispenser of information. A recent American text on the teaching of literature (Purves 1972) recommends just such a new role for the teacher. We need classroom research to enable us to describe these 'explorations' in detail. What do skilful teachers do when they explore a text with their students? What question and response strategies are apparent in their interactions with students?

7 *School literary study is best organized thematically.* I state this hypothesis here in testable form but in fact the Report does not reach such a conclusion. How best to organize the teacher-directed, whole-class strand of the literature programme remains an unresolved question. Some recommend no organization at all, a nonsequence, in just the way adults read fiction. Many schools still organize historically, or by genre.

Quite clearly, for school literary study the Report raises major questions – researchable questions – of interest to all secondary teachers of English. They are not questions which lead us to basic research in response to literature, research into the complex psycholinguistic process of reading and responding to literature, but rather into applied research, into curriculum-evaluation research, research into the effects of doing something a particular way in schools or school classrooms.

RESEARCHING THE TEACHING OF WRITING

Researchers and teachers interested in research on the teaching of writing have available several useful handbooks: the well-known guide to planning experimental, comparison-group studies (what I have been calling in this paper curriculum-evaluation studies), *Research in Written Composition* by Braddock, Lloyd-Jones, and Schoer (1963); a new review of research on the teaching of writing, *Teaching Composition: 10 Bibliographical Essays* edited by Gary Tate (1976); and a forthcoming guide to basic research on the composing process (Cooper and Odell, in press).

In referring early in the chapter on writing to the work of James Britton and his associates at the University of London, the Report directs our attention to a most significant recent development in discourse theory. From a variety of sources in linguistics, psychology, and philosophy Britton devised a scheme for classifying the kinds of writing students do in school (Britton *et al.* 1975), a scheme that has rich implications for the organization of school writing programmes and for the development of writing abilities. Britton's scheme has three broad categories: expressive, transactional and poetic. Expressive writing, which is close to informal talk, is the matrix for the others. Students move out from expressive to transactional (information-sharing, persuading) and to poetic (creating fictions). Expressive writing *remains* the matrix throughout the school years, however, even though the emphasis may shift to other kinds of writing temporarily or even exclusively in the last year or two of the secondary school. Britton's scheme was informed by another very useful system for classifying writing, that of James Moffett in *Teaching the Universe of Discourse* (1968). Moffett's system is concerned with abstraction levels in handling information and in speaker-audience relations. Moffett's abstraction levels provide the major subcategories for transactional writing in Britton's scheme. Another current discourse theory researchers should know, a theory which complements Britton's in its concern with classification by aim or function, is that of James Kinneavy (1971). All of this work gives us new ways of thinking about how we teach writing in schools and raises a host of new research questions (Odell, Cooper and Courts, in press).

As in the chapter on literary study, the research questions raised in the chapter on writing have to do with the teaching of writing to classroom groups. Once again, let me list these questions as research hypotheses that we might begin testing in classroom curriculum-evaluation studies.

1 *Language study and exercises based on that study will improve writing quality*. This hypothesis hardly seems worth stating after decades of research proving the contrary. But for some inexplicable reason many teachers still believe they are teaching writing when they are teaching students to name the parts of speech, diagram sentences, and do usage drills. The Report contains a very thoughtful discussion of this issue which ought to persuade any reader that the hypothesis as I have stated it no longer needs testing. The myth of the uses of grammar is the most tenacious one in our profession. In America the present call for a return to the basics in writing instruction unfortunately often means a return to grammar study and prescriptive usage rules.

2 *Techniques for writing are best introduced when they permit the writer to fulfil his or her own intention in writing*. There is some research supporting this hypothesis in a general way, and certainly the experience of many professional writers would support it. However, we need a great deal of further research to refine our understanding of how to advise young writers. Are there *no* general rules writers can profit from? Cannot all writers – especially younger writers – profit from learning and using discovery procedures, from sentence-combining practice, from specific revision strategies? Is the teaching of outlining to be avoided in all situations at all age levels? Is it true for all students of all ages that a 'free writing' draft is the place to begin the writing process? If techniques should be discussed only in one-to-one conferences

about a student's writing, how can these conferences best be carried out? What do teachers need to know in order to be efficient, effective conferees? What might we learn from observing the conferences of effective writing teachers, perhaps of professional writers who have become writing teachers? These few questions illustrate how much research still remains to be done on teaching methods and their timing.

3 *Sequential instruction in writing across the school years should be 'marked by an increasing differentiation in the kinds of writing a pupil can successfully tackle' and in the audiences he or she writes for.* Just on the basis of what we know about language development and discourse theory, this hypothesis seems already confirmed. But what we do not know yet is the best developmental sequence for writing tasks in different modes. Nor do we know much about what kinds of writing best prepare a student for other kinds. Is it true, as Britton claims, that expressive writing is the matrix for all other written discourse? Is dramatic writing as useful a beginning point as Moffett suggests? What do writers need to know or to practise in order to cross the bridge from written dialogue to written monologue? What is the relation between a socratic dialogue and a monological essay on the same topic? Audience is such an important concept now in discourse theory that we need to begin learning all we can about students' developing sense of audience in their writing and of the linguistic and rhetorical adjustments they must make as their sense of audience changes.

4 *Expressive writing should come from the 'continually changing context' of the student's life in and out of school, not from 'artificially stimulated and pumped up' situations provided by the teacher.* How can we connect writing to personal experience in a meaningful way? How can we encourage writing from experience and first-hand observation? How can we decrease our reliance on artificial classroom situations as contexts for writing? What do we need to know about the 'continually changing context' of adolescents' lives in order that our writing instruction can connect with it?

5 *Expressive writing and fictional writing contribute to the development of general writing ability.* Britton, Moffett, and David Holbrook (1965) would all maintain that the best way to ensure competent transactional writing at the end of the secondary school would be to build on a base of varied expressive and poetic writing across the school years. They would agree that transactional writing has its own constraints that must be learned and practised, but they would insist on a balanced writing programme with early emphasis on the expressive. This claim seems unarguable, but in fact we have no evidence to support it except Holbrook's case studies and our own hunches about the development of writing ability. We could certainly test the claim in a longitudinal curriculum-evaluation study. Perhaps more important is the question of just how it is that expressive writing contributes to general writing ability. Specifically, how does autobiographical writing enhance transactional writing?

6 *Teachers should respond first of all to the content of a piece, sometimes only to the content of the piece, and should not grade every piece.* From what we know of the composing process we could guess that it is better to respond initially to what is substantive in an early draft, rather than to what is superficial, to what Janet Emig calls the *essence* of a composition, rather than the *accidents* of its transcription. But we still need to know a great deal more about responding to student writing and about priorities for response. And we need to think further about the constraints imposed on writing instruction by the school demands of public grades and record keeping.

7 *Teachers should ask students to revise their writing.* Revision seems obviously important and yet we know very little about its practice in schools, where it may mean only recopying in ink with some superficial tidying up of transcription errors, and about its possibilities for improving writing performance. How much revising are students of different ages capable of? Is it possible that students before the stage of formal operations have difficulty taking a distanced view of their writing as an object to be manipulated, to be reconceived? Might it not be that younger students are better off writing another piece than revising a previous one?

How can we train students to revise and edit their own writing?

These hypotheses and the questions that flow from them can keep researchers busy for years. Answers to the questions are certain to improve the teaching of writing in schools.

NATIONAL MONITORING OR ASSESSMENT

The Report recommends for Britain a system of national monitoring very similar to that being carried out at present in America by the National Assessment of Educational Progress (NAEP). Since its beginning in 1977, the British system is employing varied tests of reading and writing administered in a 'light sampling' yearly to eleven and fifteen year olds. The advantage of comprehensive national assessments of reading and writing performance going on simultaneously in both countries is the critical perspective one will provide on the other. The chances of assessment becoming narrow or trivial seems less likely with continuous experimentation on both sides of the Atlantic. What is to be gained seems particularly important in the case of reading and writing. In both countries there is a sad history of incomplete and misleading measurement of these two complex psycholinguistic skills.

There are some differences between NAEP and the British system: ages of those assessed, number of age levels assessed, size of sample, structure of lay and professional committees which will construct objectives and screen test items, frequency of assessment and number of school subjects assessed, to mention the major differences. Rather than dwell on those here or describe NAEP in any detail, let me encourage interested readers to seek further information from the agencies in charge of the assessments: the National Foundation for Educational Research in Britain and the NAEP in America (details at end of paper). In a recent book John Mellon (1975) has described and evaluated the first round of NAEP assessments in English (reading, writing, literature). For either British or American readers his book is an excellent introduction to NAEP and to the problems of assessment in English.

Two brief passages in the Report nicely summarize the proposal for assessing reading and writing. Notice the concern in both passages for comprehensiveness and validity of measurement:

> (For reading) . . . the test should determine whether the child is able to extract meaning from the page. It should then assess whether he can discuss implied as well as explicit meaning, evaluate the material in terms of its own internal logic and of other evidence, and reorganize it in terms of other frames of reference. Passages would be selected for readability and calibrated for difficulty, and span a range wide enough to encompass a number of functions. These would include the descriptive, the narrative, and the expository, all within the range typically encountered by children in their school experience.
>
> (For writing) . . . writing can be adequately tested only by the scrutiny of a number of examples in which the child has to cope with a variety of demands. An important measure of success in writing is to differentiate between the styles appropriate for particular purposes. To present tasks which call upon this ability would give more complete information than could be obtained from a single assignment. For example, at eleven the monitoring procedure might include writing that is autobiographical and narrative, explanatory and descriptive. At fifteen, it should be extended to involve higher levels of abstraction and great complexity, and to include writing that answers the needs of various areas of the curriculum.

For reading assessment the Report recommends both machine-scorable multiple-choice questions and short-answer written responses, the latter to be scored by trained raters using a 'general impression' procedure. For writing assessment the Report recommends three kinds of measurement: machine-scorable tests of editing skills, counting of errors in actual writing, and general impression scoring can be highly reliable (reliability coefficients in the high 80s and low 90s) when raters are carefully trained (Britton *et al.* 1966; Cooper, in press). Education Testing Service has used it with good results for years, and NAEP uses it successfully.

One important issue discussed in the Report is the effect of large-scale testing on curriculum and on teaching practices. The writers of the Report wisely caution against an assessment that will somewhat constrain all teachers and will encourage timid or weak teachers to teach to the test. We have countless examples of the injurious effects of testing on teaching, particularly on the teaching of reading. The skills tested in reading tests based on an inadequate psychometric model of the reading process have become the skills taught in reading workbooks or the units of study in the reading class. In many American schools reading instruction is an extended exercise in testing (Robinson 1975), with students spending all their time reading quite brief selections from a workbook and then answering multiple-choice questions on the selections. An adequate notion of the reading process suggests a very different kind of instruction (Cooper and Petrosky 1976). In writing instruction, school-wide end-of-year tests emphasizing grammatical information and low-level editorial skills are still subverting the teaching of writing in many schools. In New York State, where I teach, the Regents Exam in English has had a restricting effect on English programmes in New York high schools. We know that many teachers would teach differently if the Regents Exam were either abolished or redesigned to make it more comprehensive and valid (Infantino 1974). Since testing programmes have such an impact on instruction, a really good national or state assessment would almost certainly improve instruction in schools.

SURVEYING ENGLISH TEACHING ACTIVITIES

The Report makes a most important contribution to the methodology of surveying English teaching practices. The survey instrument itself is sure to be emulated in subsequent survey studies in Britain and America. Administered at ages six, nine, twelve and fourteen, the purpose of the survey was to find out how English is being taught in British primary and secondary schools:

The survey sought information about the organization of the schools and their staffing and resources as these affected the teaching of English. It also enquired into the extent and nature of the teaching itself, with the intention of constructing a picture of the range of activities that a child might experience during a typical week at school.

Omitting discussion of the sampling procedures, I will focus on the unique features of the instrument itself, limiting myself only to the form of the instrument used at age fourteen.

Instead of asking teachers what they do in the classroom, the instrument asked teachers to describe *how one child spent a particular week in an English class.* Teachers chose the first child alphabetically from a class roll and then indicated how many minutes that child spent that week both in and out of class on writing, language study, reading, and oral English. These broad activities were further subdivided into forty-five specific activities in school and twenty-eight homework activities. For writing there are nine different types specified both for in school and for homework, three types of assignment courses, and six types of correction or response to writing by the teacher. For language the survey enquires about five different types of exercises – grammar, punctuation, vocabulary, comprehension, spelling – as well as about 'linguistics-based' language study.

Since my purpose here is not to report the findings from the survey, I will limit myself only to a few brief comments about general findings. The following are the percentages of time devoted at age fourteen to the major activities of English: oral (23), writing (23), language (22), and reading (26). One is struck by the balance of time across the four activities, and particularly by the amount of time – about half of it – devoted to the expressive language activities, talk and writing. The amount of time spent on writing is a marked increase over that found in a 1967 British survey (Squire and Applebee 1969), and is it about twice the amount of time American teachers were spending on writing in 1964 (Squire and Applebee 1969). Unless American teachers are now spending much larger amounts of time on writing – and I suspect few are – the neglect of writing demonstrated in the American survey would be part of the explanation for what many believe to be the inadequate writing performance of college students. The survey findings in the Report do indicate that teachers in Britain are making a larger place for writing instruction in English class.

Quite clearly, then, comprehensive and well-designed surveys of teaching practices can be most helpful. We are in great need of them in America at all levels – school district, state, nation. The next ones to be carried out can profit greatly from the sophisticated design of the Report's survey instrument, which is presented in its entirety in the Report.

REFERENCES

BRADDOCK, R., LLOYD-JONES, R. and SCHOER, L. (1963) *Research in Written Composition* Urbana, Illinois: National Council of Teachers of English

BRITTON, J. *et al.* (1975) *The Development of Writing Abilities (11–18)* Basingstoke, England: Macmillan Education

BRITTON, J., MARTIN, N. and ROSEN, H. (1966) *Multiple Marking of English Compositions* Schools Council Examination Bulletin No. 12 London: Her Majesty's Stationery Office

COOPER, C. R. (in press) 'Holistic evaluation of writing' in C. R. Cooper and L. Odell (Eds) *Evaluating Writing: Describing, Measuring, Judging*, Urbana, Illinois: National Council of Teachers

COOPER, C. R. and PETROSKY, A. (1976) A psycholinguistic view of the fluent reading process *Journal of Reading* 20, pp. 184–207

COOPER, C. R. (1976) Empirical studies of response to literature: review and suggestions *Journal of Aesthetic Education* 10, pp. 77–93

COOPER, C. R. (1972) *Measuring Growth in Appreciation of Literature* Newark, Delaware: International Reading Association

COOPER, C. R. and ODELL, L. (in press) *Researching Composing* Urbana, Illinois: National Council of Teachers of English

HOLBROOK, D. (1965) *English for the Rejected* New York: Cambridge University Press

INFANTINO, R. L. (1975) Results of the New York State English Council Survey on Testing *English Record* 26, pp. 4–10

KINNEAVY, J. L. (1971) *A Theory of Discourse* Englewood Cliffs, New Jersey: Prentice-Hall

MELLON, J. C. (1975) *National Assessment and the Teaching of English* Urbana, Illinois: National Council of Teachers of English

MOFFETT, J. (1968) *Teaching the Universe of Discourse* Boston: Houghton Mifflin

MONSON, D. L. and PELTOLA, B. J. (1976) *Research in Children's Literature: An Annotated Bibliography* Newark, Delaware: International Reading Association

ODELL, L., COOPER, C. R. and COURTS, C. (in press) 'Discourse theory: implications for research on composing' in C. R. Cooper and L. Odell (Eds) *Researching Composing* Urbana, Illinois: National Council of Teachers of English

PURVES, A. and Beach, R. (1972) *Literature and the Reader: Research in*

Response to Literature, Reading Interests and the Teaching of Literature Urbana, Illinois: National Council of Teachers of English

PURVES, A. (1972) *How Porcupines Make Love: Notes on a Response-Centred Curriculum* Lexington, Massachusetts: Xerox College Publishers

ROBINSON, H. M. (1975) 'Insights from research: children's behaviour while reading' in W. D. Page (Ed.) *Help for the Reading Teacher: New Directions in Research* Urbana, Illinois: National Council of Teachers of English

SMITH, F. (1971) *Understanding Reading* New York: Holt, Rinehart and Winston

SQUIRE, J. R. and APPLEBEE, R. K. (1969) *Teaching English in the United Kingdom* Urbana, Illinois: National Council of Teachers of English

SQUIRE, J. R. and APPLEBEE, R. K. (1968) *High School English Instruction Today* New York: Appleton-Century Crofts

TATE, G. (Ed.) (1976) *Teaching Composition: 10 Bibliographical Essays* Fort Worth, Texas: Texas Christian University Press

NAEP (National Assessment of Educational Progress) 700 Lincoln Tower, 1860 Lincoln Street, Denver, Colorado 80203

NFER (National Foundation for Educational Research in England and Wales) The Mere, Upton Park, Slough SL1 2DQ

Bullock and beyond: research on the writing process

Donald H. Graves

Most American teachers and children would be doing different things in classrooms tomorrow if the Bullock Committee's recommendations were put into full practice. Teachers would put aside their manuals and focus on the intentions of learners. Such items as story-starters, artificial assignments or skills instruction unallied to learner need would soon disappear. Children, on the other hand, would be encouraged to discover a sense of voice in their own writing. This would take priority over techniques.

A Language for Life is learner centred. Its recommendations are deceptively simple, yet complex when teachers attempt to apply the principles beneath them. The recommendations depend on teachers 'reading out' from the information provided by children before considering teaching approaches. Methods, techniques and objectives all emanate from information provided by the child. Recommendations 125 and 126 in the Report are examples of this stance:

125 The teacher should extend the pupil's ability as a writer primarily by developing his *intentions* (my italics) and then by working on techniques appropriate to them.
126 Progress in writing throughout the school years should be marked by an increasing differentiation in the kinds of writing a pupil can successfully tackle.

The Bullock Committee did not provide systematic research citations for each recommendation. Nor did it need to. The writing practice encouraged is, however, based on sound language theory and research.

The strength of *A Language for Life* is in its stance and direction. Its weakness is in the need for specifics, especially in writing.

In effect the Report has given us a Lewis and Clark commission but has left out the maps and compasses needed to explore a vast, uncharted territory. It has pointed us in the right direction but has left the critical work to other researchers. For example, the Report has asked teachers to attend to developmental levels of children as well as to develop their intentions. Teachers confronted with children on the morrow have the right to ask, 'Well, how do you know where a child is developmentally in order to know next steps?' and, 'What are intentions and how do you develop them?' Peter Medway (1975) has rightfully pointed to the lack of provision for the latter issue:

> Bullock says it, but only in a few places, in particular contexts, and without realizing its full import: 'Competence in language comes above all through its purposeful use . . .' (summary 128). The business of having a purpose, or intention when you talk, write or read is obviously at the centre of it. 'The teacher who aims to extend the pupil's power as a writer must therefore work first upon his intentions . . .' (11.5). 'It is upon these contexts that the teacher works with a view to arousing specific *individual* intentions . . .' (11.7). Yes – and if they aren't aroused, nothing much is going to be achieved; yet Bullock says very little more about it. Purpose enters the Report in a very weak form, chiefly as a notion in the name of which completely pointless and sterile work divorced from context is objected to.

The purpose of this section is to 'map in' some of the uncharted territory, as suggested principally by my own study of seven year old children (Graves 1973). The map should include at least an indication of the critical areas in both the writing process and the developmental sequences of children's behaviours while writing. Only those portions pertaining to these issues are reported. The research should be specific to the point that teachers will know what to look for in children's behaviours in order to help them in the writing process as well as the development of their writing intentions. Since many gaps in research still exist, this section will finally outline 'next steps' needed in research to directly aid the teaching of children's writing.

The best way to gather detailed information about the writing process is to use a case-study approach. In this way information can be gathered over a broad time span and thereby make more sense of specific behaviours children may show while they are writing. On the other hand, case-study information can be gathered in the midst of larger group data on whole classrooms of children. This helps a researcher to see if large groups are doing the same things as individuals who are being closely observed.

In my study of seven year old children, several phases of information were gathered. In the first phase, large-group data were gathered on ninety-four children in four classrooms, two formal and two informal. In this phase 1,635 writings were logged for theme, type of writing, number of words, use of accompanying art, and teacher comments. In the second phase, fourteen children were observed while they were writing in their classrooms. These data could only be gathered when the children chose to write. As you can imagine I had to spend large amounts of time waiting for these special moments. In the third phase, seventeen children were asked to choose best papers from their writing folders and give reasons for their choices. They were also asked to respond to the question, 'What do you think good writers need to do well in order to write well?' In the fourth phase, full case-study information was gathered on eight children, two from each of the four classrooms in the study. These data included information from all three phases as well as parent and teacher interviews, testing, other observations, and the assembling of an educational-developmental history. Data were gathered on all four phases simultaneously over a five month period.

STUDY FINDINGS

What were the results of the study? What conclusions and recommendations could be made from these four phases of data gathering? These will now be reported along with some spelling out of useful procedures teachers can use with their own children.

Too much of our teaching involves just a review of the child's paper, which in most cases is a final product. This study certainly showed there is more to the writing process than the mere writing down of words. Indeed, if we are to understand what is happening in the process, or if we are to understand the meaning of words used, children need to be observed before, during and after their writing.

There are several phases to the writing process as well as different kinds of writers. Each type of writer has different needs in each of the writing-process phases. Data on each of these, writing process and writer types, has emerged from the study. A summary of each is contained in Figure 1 (p. 194).

The reactive writer is most often a boy and the reflective writer is most often a girl. The reactive and reflective writers, however, are each composite profiles of a general type of child. Reactive behaviours are necessary coping behaviours that children supply because of writing conditions, developmental level, or both. These characteristics exist in varying degrees in all children and can emerge under different types of writing conditions. The characteristics, however, can be seen more clearly at the high (reflective) and low (reactive) ends of a developmental scale.

But these characteristics in the two writers have practical significance for teaching. It is possible to predict what children will do in the different process phases and thereby give us opportunities to help children.

There are many points at which children can be helped. If we think of the two types of writers portrayed in Figure 1 we can clearly see that some writers are helped at some points more than others. The factors of rehearsal, spelling, voiced to unvoiced language, use of products, writing speed, idea flow are useful points to examine to determine teaching strategy.

Rehearsal

Some children do not know what they are going to write either when they are assigned a topic or when they have decided to write on their own. They need to rehearse. Rehearsal can come

FIGURE I

PROCESS PHASE	WRITER TYPES	
Precomposing (All activity prior to writing.)	*Reactive writer* Needs to rehearse ideas for writing through drawing, painting, block construction, etc. Talks and makes sounds to accompany activity. Behaviours resemble other play activity as with trucks, housekeeping, etc. Is frustrated if precomposing is not provided.	*Reflective writer* Does not need to rehearse visibly before writing. Rehearsal is going on all the time through reading, personal experiences, TV, etc.
Composing (All activity from time child writes until work is completed.)	Talks out loud or voices intermittently with writing. Writes slowly, has difficulty with spelling. Does not know beyond a sentence what will be written next. Uses drawing or precomposing materials as idea source during writing. Proofreads at word unit level only. Characters do, but do not reflect. Ideas occur in action-reaction couplets. ('He hit 'em, he hit 'em back.') Even composing behaviours resemble other play activity.	Writes rapidly and silently (8–10 wpm). Characters express feelings, reflect. Does not need a visible idea-bank to refer to. Ideas emerging in the writing are used as a bank. Child has a four to ten sentence advanced understanding of what will be written. Spells rapidly to own satisfaction. Ideas are connected.
Postcomposing (All activity after writing is completed.)	Quickly puts work away. Work was usually done for the 'doing', not as a means to a more distant end.	Child may occasionally survey work or share with another. Words may be adjusted. A few may illustrate after the work is completed. Depending on the environment, child may know where the work will be placed – display, collection, bound, etc.

in many forms: block play, painting, construction, conversation, or drawing being the most common. If a teacher asks a child who needs to rehearse before writing, 'Tell me, what are you going to write next, or do next?', the child will respond, 'I don't know', or, 'I need to draw the picture first'. If the children who need rehearsal don't get it, writing becomes almost an impossible task. They rely heavily both on the working out of meaning through graphics, a more concrete image, as well as a source of visible information when they enter into the composing phase. These are the very children who are often left in 'the dust'. Later, when these children become adults they do not feel able to write the most minimal of communications, even a three sentence 'excuse' note to their child's teacher. At first (ages six to seven) they are not aware of the difficulty in composing in writing, but soon (if the rehearsal question is not observed) they are aware of being behind other children and lose whatever 'intentions' might have been theirs. These are the children Peter Medway is referring to in his critique of the Bullock Report: 'They exemplify what is achieved by this sort of teaching that doesn't see getting the pupils involved as a major problem; and it doesn't lead to language development – not to any degree worth writing home about.' A teacher who provides for rehearsal through a wide range of media has visible proof of 'intention' and better knows, therefore, how to add power through questions and encouragement to the child's first sense of authority.

Is it not also clear that expression in one media form lays a base for expression in other areas such as writing? In environments where the *only* form of expression is in writing, writing suffers.

More advanced children (reflective), on the other hand, are in a constant state of rehearsal. How else can a child leave one activity, pick up paper and pencil, and within ten seconds begin to write rapidly? Furthermore, if they are asked what they are going to write next, they tend to reply with a full paragraph of information. Children who are in such a state of rehearsal often need longer time periods in which to complete their writings. Set time periods for writing, either for reflective or reactive writers, penalize both.

Overt and covert language

Some children subvocalize when they first attempt to read to themselves. That is, they pronounce the words to themselves as they are read. Children do the same when they write and the effect of such behaviour is clearly seen in the seven year old study.

First, when subvocalizers compose they make ten times as many spelling errors as those who do not. It would appear that the effective use of inner language (when no outer language is visible) is strongly linked to spelling. I hypothesised that since the child can more effectively represent ideas to himself through inner language, there is less conflict in the actual production of the word through writing. Secondly, children who subvocalize write half as slowly and must reread to find their place five times as often as children who use no external language when composing.

Teachers who know that overt language interferes with the composing process can help those children who *must* use it. Children use it for a reason and need extra time, encouragement, and rehearsal to aid their composing. When such developmental factors are overlooked in the 'all-class' writing assignment for a set period of forty minutes such children are penalized. The seeds are sown for the ruination of the intentions of children who might otherwise enjoy writing. The profile of the person who later will be disenfranchised from literacy emerges with greater clarity.

Idea flow

Reactive writers do not have much advanced sense of what they will be composing, whether they are drawing or composing with words. If the question is asked, 'Tell me, what are you going to be writing next', or, 'and then what will happen?' reactive children (at the age of seven) do not respond beyond one to two sentences from what they are working on at the moment.

Reflective writers, on the other hand, have a well-developed sense at age seven of what will happen next in their composing. On request they are capable of relating the entire message they have but begun to compose.

Teachers who are sensitive to these differences in writers can develop the intention of the reactive writer through skilful, periodic questions: 'Tell me, what will Tommy do next? How do you suppose his friend, Charles, will feel then? What are some good words that will tell how he feels?'

Reflective writers can be pushed harder at their points of information: 'I see that you are writing about bird feeders. Now you have spoken about types of feeders, but you really haven't said much about their locations or the types of feed for different birds. How well do you think someone will be able to feed birds from what you have written here?'

SUMMARY

The writing component of the Bullock Report is based on sound language theory and research. It is a learner-centred Report with focus given to the importance of considering children's intentions in writing as well as their developmental differences. More specifics are needed, however, if teachers are to use the Report as a basis for action with children. A third area, writing process, not even mentioned in the Report, needs to be brought in to go with the emphases on development and intentions.

Until recently research has not provided the information needed to deal with these issues. Descriptions of products, controlled methodological studies, or studies in correlation are too far removed from reporting what children actually do to be of help to us. That is, children simply have not been observed when they are engaged in the writing process in the broadest sense. On the other hand, this is precisely what teachers have to do from day to day. They observe what children are doing and then decide what they must do next to help them.

If the recommentations of the Bullock Report were taken seriously, more demands than ever would be placed on teachers' capacities to observe children. The study of seven year old children provides information that will help them in that very area. It provides specific help in observation, plus a view of different kinds of children as they function in the three phases of the writing process: precomposing, composing and postcomposing.

Such specific behaviours as rehearsal, uses of overt and covert language (especially as they relate to spelling, rereading, and writing speed) and idea flow are reported under two general types of writers, reactive and reflective. The meaning of these data are interpreted as they would aid or detract from developing the intentions of young writers.

NEEDED RESEARCH

The map for the writing process and the developmental profiles of young children has been barely sketched in. We have some sense of anatomy – the ingredients involved. We have practically no sense of physiology – the functioning of children as they write. We have not even approached the age of alchemy with our understanding. Indeed, the Romans knew more about the anatomy and physiology of humans than we know about the anatomy and physiology of the writing process as engaged in by children.

Where then should research on children's writing begin? I believe the following ventures ought to receive priority:

1   Observe the composing of children in the broadest sense in order to understand the sequence of developmental steps involved in writing.
2   Develop new tools and practitioners for investigating the writing processes of children.

Observation and developmental sequencing

In most research circles it would be unthinkable to speculate about human behaviour without actually observing it. The composing of children should be no exception. Jean Piaget could hardly have done his work without a systematic and meticulous observation of children. The fruit of his work has made some of the most fundamental and significant changes in teaching.

Although some work has been started in the observations of the composing of seven year old children, data is needed on other ages from the time they first begin to represent in scribbling until at least ten to twelve years of age (indeed, we need them well beyond the childhood years). In this way overlapping data will provide developmental sequences on important variables. Some important variables have been identified. Further investigation will reveal many more that will give specific help to teachers. Some variables needing further investigation are:

198

1   *Sex, differences in young writers* Preliminary evidence shows
    these to be highly significant. Boys and girls appear to need
    help unique to their own sex.
2   *Overt language* Further investigation of external language in a
    variety of situations should help us to understand the develop-
    mental function of inner language. Such evidence should help
    us explain early spelling, idea flow, and composing strategies.
3   *Reading and writing process* Writing behaviours need to be
    observed along with reading behaviours to further under-
    stand the processes of each and the developmental relation-
    ship of one to the other.
4   *Different environments* Children need to be observed in a
    variety of settings, especially in those where writing is
    apparently going well. In this way case studies will aid us in
    describing what best affects the intentions of young writers.
    We need to know what affects their sense of voice and
    authority as well as the place of writing in their overall
    schemes of communication.

NEW PRACTITIONERS AND TOOLS

Right now there are not many people engaged in the actual
observation of children while they are writing, either for research
purposes or for instructional assessment in the schools. Part of
the reason is that systematic preparation for skilled observation
is not often provided by universities or the public domain. People
in education usually have to cross over to departments of
psychology or anthropology for such skills and then adapt them
for use with children. They are needed as much by teachers as
they are by researchers. Something has to be done.

Finally, in addition to direct observation skills, new tools are
needed to augment basic data-gathering. For example, video
tape recordings may help us to view the full range of verbal and
nonverbal language used in composing. Or the electric pen
designed by Professor James Britton with the help of engineers;
such a pen will record the words a child composes on another
sheet of paper with the exact time recorded for each word operation.

Consistent with the Bullock Report's emphasis, most of the
focus on research needs in this report is placed on the gathering

of more knowledge about children. Too often we have presumed to know how or why they compose and how we can help them. Their intentions are lost in the shuffle as is the joy of writing.

REFERENCES

DES (1975) *A Language for Life* (The Bullock Report) London: Her Majesty's Stationery Office

GRAVES, D. H. (1973) Children's Writing: Research Directions and Hypotheses based upon an Examination of the Writing Processes of Seven Year Old Children. Doctoral Dissertation, State University of New York at Buffalo

MEDWAY, P. (1975) 'How it looks from here' in H. Rosen, (Ed.) *Language and Literacy in Our Schools* London: University of London Institute of Education

Action-research: a description with examples

Robert P. Parker, Jnr

Through the grades in American schools, those who teach are not those who do research on teaching. Most research on teaching is conducted by outside 'experts' who come in from colleges, universities, and public and private agencies – only occasionally at the behest of the school or school system. True, some larger American districts do have research offices staffed by these same kinds of 'experts', though their research activities usually are either partly or totally evaluative. That is, they administer standardized achievement tests at regularly scheduled times each year in order to find out how well certain knowledges and skills are being taught by that system in relation to national norms, or by individual schools in that system in comparison with other schools.

These school-based research people seldom make systematic enquiries into teaching/learning processes, nor do they often see themselves as people whose job it is to help train teachers to enquire into such processes, either individually or collaboratively. In effect then, teachers and the schools they teach in are the objects rather than the agents of research. At the same time, teachers are also supposed to be the consumers of research, though, as Charles Cooper points out earlier in this section, many English teachers continue to ignore research findings which indicate clearly that increases in grammatical knowledge are unrelated to improvement in writing performance.

On the whole, few teachers pay much attention to research and, when they do, they frequently complain about their difficulty in knowing what is significant and what is trivial, as well as in applying what seems to be significant in their teaching. So, not only are researching and teaching separate activities conducted by separate groups of educators, but also the outcomes of research remain pretty much separate from conventional teaching practices.

Why does this traditional separation exist and why does it continue? Some people have argued that it exists, and continues, because preservice teacher-training programmes do not teach prospective teachers how to read research and apply relevant findings. This argument seems true, but trivial. In my view, teachers do not read and apply research findings mainly because the entire socialization process of their training 'teaches' them to be practitioners and not practitioner/researchers. We have created a cult of specialization for educational research, currently dominated by the psychologists and statisticians, just as we have developed a cult of specialization for educational administration. In both cases, the separate training programmes and separate credentialling procedures lead to separate, and higher, status niches in the educational hierarchy. And to fully mythologize this separateness and specialness of status, a mystique of special expertise has developed which makes it appear as if these are the only people who can do the jobs of administration or research. Obviously, so teachers think, they would have to go through all the training that the researchers went through before they could do research.

I would argue that one only becomes interested in reading research when one is doing research. Doing research oneself creates a purpose for attending to research that others are doing. After all, researchers read research, and teachers read narrative accounts about teaching, though not *vice versa*. And why not? It makes sense. What doesn't make sense though is the belief many teachers have that they are not qualified to do research, that research must be left to the 'experts'. To this I reply, 'Baloney! If you feel this way, you've been had, sold a bill of goods intended to keep you in your place.'

After all, in fields like medicine, dentistry, optometry, psychiatry, it has always been fairly common for some practitioners also to be researchers. Many such health professionals regularly do experimental or clinical or descriptive research as a part of their ongoing professional life and activities. I want teachers likewise to do research regularly as a part of their ongoing professional life and activities. Obviously, this research will have to be practical and context specific. That is, it will have to be aimed at results which will improve teaching/learning arrangements in the particular setting in which they work. To describe this kind of research, I have borrowed the term 'action-research' from the social sciences.[1]

ACTION-RESEARCH: A DEFINITION

I see action-research as a loose, informal, fluid kind of enterprise, unique because of where it takes place (the context), who does it (the researchers), why they do it (the purpose), what they do (the activities), and what happens with the outcomes, rather than because the investigators use any special methods of enquiry. Action-research is unique also because it is 'not simply a programme of action with a built-in form of evaluation, but consists of a complicated interplay between action and research at all points'.

1 *Context*

Action-research takes place in a normal work context, in this case a school, where a particular job, teaching, is being done that is regularly done there. It does not take place in a separate laboratory: rather, the work setting becomes, in part or at times, the laboratory and those working in it begin to assume an 'experimental' stance towards their work. That is, they begin to view the setting for their work, their clients, and their own work activities, as open to investigation. They see that they can study these features of their work life in some way so as to learn more about them, and thus control them in more informed and purposeful ways.

2 *Purpose*

The normal purpose of the job, and the job tasks and job roles, coexist in some kind of dynamic relationship with the research purposes as they are conceived by those operating the job roles and tasks. The research purposes are kept 'in mind' and have, hopefully, their own integrity, but they are embedded in, are coordinated with and adapted to, the demands of the job. This coordination may at first be intuitive but will, over time, tend to be made more explicit and logical. Overall, the research purpose is to discover something – some data – about the normal job operations which will document and inform, and therefore confirm or alter, these operations.

3 *Activities*

The research purposes, because they exist in their own right, and because there is an intent to make them operative, are apt to require some experiments with or on normal job operations. These purposes, because they are research purposes, also require that the experiments eventually take on a systematic character, a logical structure, which carries out the intent of the enquiry. They cannot be completely *ad hoc* or separate, either in relation to the normal work operations or in relation to whatever theory is being used as a framework for conceptualizing the enquiry or analysing the results.

I might say also that, by my definition, the investigative activities cannot be external or *post hoc* either. Standardized examinations given periodically cannot be a part of action-research, nor is, for example, a grammar proficiency examination given by a secondary English department at the end of tenth grade. These enquiries are discrete, occasional, and after the fact rather than embedded in the daily operations of teachers. Also, they are evaluative and thus lack the more open and exploratory stance required for action-research.

4 *Outcomes*

Because the research purposes and activities are embedded in the normal job purposes and activities, the outcomes they yield *along the way* will be analysed and interpreted in the light of normality and will be seen, in the first instance, as having implications for that normality. The main questions in an educational setting will be ones like the following: 'How do these outcomes relate to my teaching and that of my colleagues? What do they suggest we might do in the way of strengthening or altering normal practice?' So the outcomes are, in a sense, immediately put back into practice in that setting, though both the theory and the research procedures may be altered in the process. Only secondarily will the outcomes be seen in relation to other settings. In fact, there may have to be an outside person on the research 'team' to urge dissemination of the outcomes beyond the immediate setting.

Unquestionably, we are at a point in time when great public concern with standards of literacy is being voiced in both England and America. The publication of the Bullock Report alone gives evidence of this concern in England, and the recent spate of publicity about alleged declines in the writing ability of young Americans documents this concern on our side of the Atlantic. Whether standards of literacy, particularly in writing, are actually declining in either country, it seems clear that large segments of the educated public think they are and that, at least for America, the decline has reached crisis proportions.

In preparing its recommendations for assessing 'standards of achievement in literacy' in British schools, the Bullock Committee wisely acknowledged that 'no system of monitoring can encompass all the various objectives in English promoted by a wide variety of schools, let alone all the individual teachers within them'. In their view, the 'ideal system' of monitoring would 'employ new instruments to assess a wider range of attainments than has been attempted in the past' and would 'allow new criteria to be established for the definition of literacy'.

Social change inevitably brings with it changing demands for literacy among citizens, as well as new ideas about the definition and teaching of literacy in schools. Just as inevitably, there will be tensions between these new definitions and approaches and conventional, sometimes nostalgic, ideas about what society has always required for literate functioning by its members. In the Bullock Report, this tension is implied in the shuttling between those who emphasize young people actively taking the process of learning to talk, write, read, and listen in hand *for* themselves and *in* their own ways, and those who favour the direct teaching of specific, isolated literacy skills to young people in set sequences.

In America, where more and more states are adopting legislation calling for continuous assessment of students' levels of minimum competency achievement in reading, writing, and mathematics, the important threat is that these competencies and the tests for them will be designed by nonschool people who are more familiar with test design than with the learning processes of different kinds of students or the goals of various schools. If this happens, the tests will probably not be new, or at least not newly conceptualized, nor will they assess a 'wider range of attainments than has been attempted in the past'. And it is even less likely that these tests will 'allow new criteria to be established for the definition of literacy'.

It is in this context of the continuous monitoring of literacy that I want to describe the Schools Council/University of London Writing Across the Curriculum Project as an example of vital and successful action-research.

This Project arose from, and attempted to apply the findings of, an earlier (1966–71) research project on the development of writing abilities in school students aged 11–18 (Britton 1975). It was funded by the Schools Council, which had also funded the research, as a development project, and its aims were to consider school practice regarding the use of writing in various areas of the curriculum, to illuminate the contribution writing can make to learning in all subjects, and to find new ways of helping students to develop their writing abilities.

The Project team wrote in *Why Write?* 1973[2]:

As teachers we are interested not in the development of writers as writers, but in writing as a means of development – cognitive, affective, and social. That writing may be such a means is due to the nature of its two faces: on the one hand it looks to other people and seeks to transfer something to them by way of informing, advising, commanding, persuading, and sharing; on the other, it can also organize more clearly for the writer himself whatever perceptions he has about the world he lives in and his own relation to it. Using this second face enables him to select and hold for closer contemplation aspects of his own experience which can be scanned for particular features – sorted into logical or chronological order, re-arranged for his own satisfaction, invested with particular feelings and so on. This process of personal selection, contemplation and differentiation is very important, because it *changes the writer*, he is a different person when he has done it, because now he has articulated a feeling or a thought or an attitude more clearly, or seen how a bit of his experience fits into the pattern which he is gradually building up for himself; in other words, he is more conscious than he was. It is these processes which can go on in writing which can make it so powerful in an educational sense.

To put this philosophy into practice, and to carry out the aims listed above, the Project team elected to work with teachers in the following ways:

1   by collaborating with teachers in schools, in varying degrees of association, from shared teaching to postal consultations
2   by having discussions with teachers as widely as possible through conferences, seminars and workshops
3   and by publishing a variety of working papers, discussion documents and bulletins.

The general working process of the Project is presented in the diagram on page 208.

In this example of action-research, the impetus for enquiry and experimentation came, in most cases, from discussions the Project team had with teachers. Nonetheless, the team's aim always was to encourage teachers, in the light of the theory and research findings it presented, to examine their own ideas and practices about writing. The team hoped that this examination would lead teachers to devise their own experiments with language teaching and to share the results of these experiments with other faculties in their school and with the team.

At the same time, the team members were writing discussion papers on their own, drawing on materials sent in by teachers which illuminated or extended important aspects of the original theory. These longer, more theoretical papers were discussed by the team at their meetings, revised, and published in pamphlets.[3] In fact, though, only the first four pamphlets were written entirely by team members. Twice, interested groups of teachers who had been experimenting actively with writing in their classes came together with the team for an intensive weekend of discussion and writing. Out of the first weekend, a meeting with a group of science teachers, came *Writing in Science*; out of the second, a meeting with a group of humanities teachers, came *Language and Learning in the Humanities*. Although team members contributed individual papers to these pamphlets and did

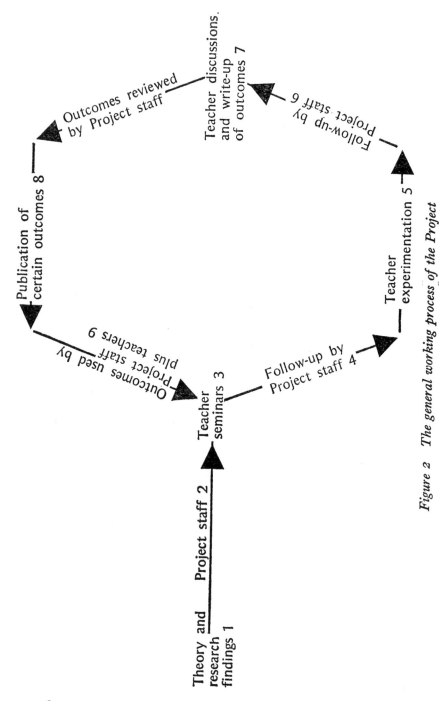

208

Figure 2   The general working process of the Project

1 The theory and research findings are from Stage One of the research project.[3] The original research team consisted of James Britton, Director; Nancy Martin, Dr Harold Rosen, Tony Burgess, Denis Griffiths, Bernard Newsome, and Alex McLeod.

2 During the 1974-5 academic year the Project staff included Nancy Martin, Director: Bryan Newton, Pat D'Arcy, and Dr Robert Parker Jnr. Previous Project staff included Harold Smith and Peter Medway.

3 Each seminar involved a new group of teachers, a new constituency, so the circle of teachers involved in the Project widened consistently.

4 In certain cases, a Project staff member would, on request, follow-up the workshop by visiting a particular school to assist interested teachers in sharpening the focus of their discussions and experiments.

5 This experimentation might include widening the range of audience or functions for writing within a particular class, across classes, or between two different schools. It might alternatively, or in addition, involve teachers of various subjects in discussions of writing (or language) across the curriculum.

6 In a few interested schools, where a lot of experimental work was going on, a Project staff member attached himself to that school. He or she visited the school regularly (perhaps once a week) and met with teachers to discuss their experiments, make suggestions and gather interim material for the entire Project staff to discuss.

7 Some teachers involved themselves in writing up the outcomes of their experiments. On several occasions this was accomplished by bringing teachers from different schools together for an intensive weekend of discussion and writing.

8 These written materials were collected and reviewed by the Project staff, and with some selectivity and occasional light editing, were organized and prepared for publication in either packs or pamphlets. The packs were built around students' work and had a practical orientation. These new materials, published and unpublished, were used immedi-

ately by Project staff members in workshops with teachers.

9 As certain teachers became knowledgeable about the theory and skilled in working with teachers, they were invited to participate with the Project staff in leading workshops. Thus, teachers were soon teaching each other, both directly through workshops and indirectly through the published results of their discussions and classroom work. Thus, also, there was an ever growing group of teachers whose ideas and whose teaching were being touched in some way by the work of the Project.

---

the editorial preparation for publication, the majority of papers in each collection were written by teachers.

Because the team saw the packs as ephemeral, they were given away free and not reprinted. The pamphlets, on the other hand, were sold and the money used to reprint them when necessary. As with the packs, the pamphlets were sent to people on the Project mailing list and used as discussion materials at conferences.

Finally, before the Project ended in August 1976, the then current team wrote a book entitled *Writing and Learning: Across the Curriculum 11–16* (Martin *et al.* 1976). This book presented the teams' views about their work on writing with teachers of all subjects and concluded with a discussion of what the team saw as key issues emerging from their work and needing further investigation. Hopefully, these issues will be some of the ones around which action-research on writing for learning across the curriculum will continue. If so, the Schools Council's money and the Project team's five years of work will bear further fruit.

At this point, you may well ask: 'What are specific action-research projects that others have done or that I might be doing?' I would answer that question by drawing first on my experience with the Writing across the Curriculum Project and second on certain recommendations in the Bullock Report which lend themselves to this kind of enquiry.

It is useful to begin by looking about at what already goes on in your school, by doing an informal status survey of some aspect of literacy teaching in your immediate situation. You might ask your colleagues to describe what they think distinguishes a good writer from a poor one. From these descriptions you can build up a profile of the views operative in your school. How much unanimity is there, or how much diversity? What are people's views across subjects, if your school is specialized by subjects? These profiles can be discussed as part of an inservice programme. Next, you could ask your colleagues to identify a good writer and a poor writer in their classes, to collect several samples of each pupil's writing, and to bring these samples together for examination and discussion. What happens if some people disagree about what is good writing and what is poor writing? What does this mean for pupils? Or, you might ask your colleagues what they think writing is *for* in schools, what purpose it generally serves. If they will write down their views, you can collect them, categorize them, and prepare a discussion report for a faculty meeting.

A more ambitious project would be to select a sample group of students within a single grade, or across two or more grades, and collect all the writing that each pupil does in all subjects for a period of three to six weeks. When the sample is complete, a small group of teachers can analyse the writing by asking such questions as: *How much* original composing are these pupils doing, as compared with drill work, filling in blanks, or entering short answers to set questions? *What kinds* of writing are they doing? *What kinds of audiences* do they have in mind for their writing? *What purposes* do they seem to be writing for? Does any of the writing aid them in new learning, or is most of the writing done to show teachers what they have already learned? What kinds of grading practices do they encounter? What does their experience of writing seem to be teaching them about *how* one writes in school, what one writes *for* in school, and what happens to school writing when it is 'finished'? Is there any evidence to suggest that any of these pupils will like writing enough to become 'life-long' writers? While these investigative activities may, quite naturally, be unsystematic at first, the need to make sense of the collected information will eventually result in more carefully organized research as well as a search for more powerfully explanatory theory. There will be a true process of learning by doing.

So far, my suggestions for action-research projects have focused on writing, partly because the primary data, pupils' writing, is more concrete than that produced by talking or listening or reading. Yet, as the Bullock Report (p. 515) concludes: 'Language competence grows incrementally, through an interaction of writing, talk, reading, and experience, and the best teaching deliberately influences the nature and quality of this growth.'

What, then, can you do to investigate the relationships among these other uses of language, especially as they are currently being 'influenced' by the practices and materials in your school? First, you will probably have to begin by looking at them separately. To investigate the uses of talk for learning, you might tape-record pupils discussing new material in different sizes and kinds of groups: whole class and small groups, teacher-directed and student-directed, and so on. Using the analysis which Mike Torbe presented in his article as a guide, you can then transcribe the tapes and examine the transcripts to see how the pupils' learning through discussion is affected by the different groups. For example: In which groups do pupils control a greater share of the total 'air time'? In which groups do pupils ask more total questions? In which groups do they ask more 'open' questions – questions which require thinking and have no particular right or wrong answers? In which groups do they work more consistently towards understanding new material in their own terms as compared with simply taking over the linguistic formulations presented by the teacher or the textbook? If a teacher joins or leaves a discussion while it is in progress, what happens to the *learning content* of the discussion? What relationships seem to exist between certain kinds of discussion groups and performance on different kinds of tests?

You might examine the more complicated relationships among talking, reading, and writing by designing ways of gathering data to answer questions like the following: Do students read with greater comprehension when they discuss the topic of the reading material beforehand? If so, why is this the case? If not, why not? Is this equally true for fictional as well as factual reading? Does discussion after reading aid comprehension? What kinds of discussions are most helpful? Is pupils' writing better when they discuss what they are going to write about before they begin? Is this true for all students? For all types (modes) of writing? Do students revise their writing more effectively (more fully) when they discuss their rough drafts with teachers? With peers?

Obviously, these are only a very few of the many possible questions that might give rise to action-research projects. You will have to begin with your own questions, those which have priority in your situation, and you will have to experiment with how you ask them in order to be able to design informal research activities around them. And even when you are enthusiastic and willing to do something, some of your colleagues will say they are too busy with lesson planning, record keeping and marking students' work to bother with any kind of research. Others will claim that they are just not qualified.

The starting point for such teachers is to encourage them to consider a new way of thinking about their operations as teachers. How can they teach so as to continually learn more about their teaching? Already they are getting and interpreting feedback from their pupils; the issue, then, involves their deciding whether to structure their teaching so that this feedback is more probing, more systematic and more generalized to the entire school, instead of just being idiosyncratic, occasional and exclusive to them as individuals. The Bullock Report urges that we think of our teaching as involving a constant 'interplay between action and research at all points'.

In our view, teachers should be involved not only in experimenting with the outcomes of research but also in identifying the problems, setting up hypotheses, and carrying out the collection and assessment of data. We are glad to see that such enterprises are already taking place in some colleges and university institutes of education in workshop courses as part of inservice training. This kind of participation can help teachers to a better understanding of the discipline, methods, and limitations of research, and can ensure that the outcomes are put to practical use. We should particularly like to see more action-research in which teachers are widely involved, for we believe that this form of activity holds considerable promise for the development of new practices in school. (p. 553)

This approach to teaching would, among other things, put teachers in a better position to make productive decisions about their real needs for growth and change, especially at a time when the national stress is falling more heavily on inservice and continuing education in all professions. It would also put teachers in a better position when they discuss school programmes and their effectiveness with boards of education and parents. They will have information which they understand and care about because they have gathered it themselves in relation to questions they really want to answer.

REFERENCES

BRITTON, J. et al. (1975) *The Development of Writing Abilities 11–18* Basingstoke, England: Macmillan Education

MARTIN, N., D'ARCY, P., NEWTON, B. and PARKER, R. (1976) *Writing and Learning Across the Curriculum 11–16* London: Ward Lock Educational

NOTES

1 DES (1970) *Educational Priorities* (Halsey Report) London: Her Majesty's Stationery Office
2 See note 3 below
3 These pamphlets, all published jointly by the Schools Council and the University of London Institute of Education were: *From Information to Understanding, Why Write?, From Talking to Writing, Keeping Options Open, Writing in Science* and *Language and Learning in the Humanities.* They are all now available from Ward Lock Educational.

The contributors

Charles Cooper has taught for twenty years in secondary schools and universities. Active in the National Council of Teachers of English, he has been a member of the Editorial Board, and he is presently chairman of the research committee and a member of the editorial board of Research in the Teaching of English. He teaches in the Graduate English Education Program in the Faculty of Educational Studies at the State University of New York, Buffalo, New York. His research interests are in the nature of written language and the composing processes and in measurement and evaluation problems generally in English education.

Chris Crowest, formerly Principal Lecturer in Primary Education at Dartford College of Education, has recently been appointed to the post of Senior Inspector for Primary Education in the Inner London Education Authority. He completed his studies in primary education at London University and was headmaster of primary schools in Sevenoaks and Beckenham, Kent, before becoming a college lecturer. He has written plays for broadcasting and has edited children's textbooks, but sees himself essentially as a general practitioner primary teacher.

Frances R. A. Davis, formerly Assistant Professor of Preschool Education and Child Psychology, is presently Project Coordinator for the Title XX, Brooklyn College (CUNY) Day Care Staff Development Project. She is the author of journal articles dealing with language, symbolic development and special education problems. Since 1972 she has spent several summers in England during which time she directed internship programmes for American college students and teachers, and conducted research in children's narrative assessment.

Donald H. Ecroyd, Professor of Speech and Education at Temple

University, is past-President of the Eastern Communication Association. He is the author or co-author of eleven textbooks in speech communication. He is active in research dealing with the relationship of language learning and communication pedagogy, and worked with the Research Board of the Speech Communication Association in the development of the 1972 Memphis Conference on teacher training. He was one of the principal researchers participating in the SCA's national project on Speech Communication Competencies (1973–6), and is one of the four ERIC-commissioned co-authors preparing TRIPS (Theory and Research into Practice) booklets based upon that project.

Donald Graves, formerly an elementary teacher and principal, is Associate Professor in Early Childhood Education at the University of New Hampshire. He serves as Research Editor of *Language Arts*, conducts research on the writing process with young children, and is Director of the Writing Process Laboratory at the University of New Hampshire. His articles have appeared in such journals as *Language Arts* and *Research in Teaching of English*.

Eleanore T. Kenney has been Director of The Miriam School, St Louis, Missouri, since 1959. She is the author of publications dealing with special education, with particular focus on children with normal intellectual potential who have emotional and/or learning disabilities, including those with 'Specific Learning Disabilities'. As a part of Miriam School's expanding community outreach programme, she has been involved in many aspects of teacher training and school consultation in the Greater St Louis area. During the past three years she has been in-service practicum coordinator and consultant to the Developmental Learning Program in the St Louis City Schools. Her articles have appeared in the *American Journal of Orthopsychiatry*, *American Journal of Mental Deficiency*, and *Exceptional Children*.

Ramon Minovi has taught English to students of all ages from six to sixty in primary schools, secondary schools, and through adult education. He is currently Head of the English Department in Sir Wilfrid Martineau School, Birmingham, England.

An enthusiastic member of the National Association for the Teaching of English, he chairs the Birmingham Branch of NATE and edits its Newsletter. He is the author or co-author of a number of articles and of a book, *Early Reading and Writing*, published in 1976.

Kathryn Madera Miller, formerly a home economics and nursery school teacher, is an Associate Professor of Child Development in the College of Home Economics at Iowa State University in Ames, Iowa. She presently coordinates the nursery school, extended day and kindergarten laboratories and teaches in the areas of curriculum and administration of programmes for children and current issues in child care. Mrs Miller is the author of articles on the British infant school in *Childhood Education*. Open education, teacher education, and working with parents are other professional interests.

Bryan Newton taught in secondary schools for ten years. From 1974–6 he was Project Officer on the Schools Council/London University Institute of Education 'Writing Across the Curriculum' Project and is joint author of the project book *Writing and Learning Across the Curriculum 11–16*. He was on the faculty of the National Endowment for the Humanities Summer Institute on 'Writing in the Learning of Humanities' held at Rutgers University, New Jersey, in 1977. He is at present advisory teacher in reading and language development in Essex.

Robert Parker taught English in secondary schools in Maryland and Illinois for several years. After completing his Ph.D. in the School of Education at Northwestern University, he taught beginning teachers at the University of Chicago for two years before moving to Rutgers University where he teaches experienced teachers. He is the author of several articles and the co-author of two previous books: *Teaching English in Secondary School* and *Writing and Learning Across the Curriculum 11–16*.

Frederick J. G. Poole, Headmaster, Amherst County Primary School, Sevenoaks, Kent, and previously of Northchapel Junior School, West Sussex, has a Diploma in Child Development from the University of London Institute of Education. He is the author of *Some Aspects of Parents' Involvement in Schools*, London Institute of Education Library, 1973.

Margaret Roberts is currently Senior Lecturer in Child Development at the University of London Institute of Education. Before that she taught in nursery and infant schools and was involved in teacher training in the United Kingdom, Australia, and Canada. Her interests include young children's thinking, symbolic representation and interactions with people and things.

Mike Torbe is presently Curriculum Development Officer for Coventry. Previously he taught in primary and secondary schools and a college of education. He has written several articles about English teaching and language, was one of the authors of *Understanding Children Writing* and edited, with Robert Protherough, *Classroom Encounters: Language and English Teaching*. He is on the editorial board of *English in Education*, the journal of the National Association for the Teaching of English, and is the author of the Association's pamphlet *Language across the Curriculum: Guidelines for Schools*.

Jean Tough was formerly a primary school teacher and a lecturer in a college of education. She is now Senior Lecturer in Education in the School of Education at the University of Leeds. She directs an advanced course of study for experienced qualified teachers, leading to the Diploma in Primary Education. She has undertaken research into children's development and use of language and now directs the Schools Council, Communication Skills in Early Childhood Project, and its extension, Seven to Eleven. She is the author of several articles on language in primary education and the following books: *Focus on Meaning*, *The Development of Meaning*, *Listening to Children Talking*, *Talking and Learning*.

Index